Connacht Coastal Run

A running and sometimes walking adventure around the western coastline of Ireland

Gerry O'Boyle

Copyright © 2024 Gerry O'Boyle
All Rights Reserved.

978-1-915502-87-2

All intellectual property rights including copyright, design right and publishing rights rest with the author. No part of this publication may be copied, reproduced, stored, or transmitted in any way including any written, electronic, recording or photocopying without written permission of the author and the content is for your personal use and enjoyment only. The author does not assume liability for loss or damage caused by errors or omissions. Published by Orla Kelly Publishing.

Orla Kelly Publishing
27 Kilbrody,
Mount Oval,
Rochestown,
Cork,
Ireland

"There's nothing more beautiful than the way the ocean refuses to stop kissing the shoreline, no matter how many times it's sent away."

Sarah Kay

*All Profits from this book go to
Rosedale Special School in Galway City.*

Contents

Stages	County	Start	Finish	Page
41	Sligo	Bundoran	Grange	15
42	Sligo	Grange	Drumcliff	19
43	Sligo	Drumcliff	Sligo Town	23
44	Sligo	Sligo Town	Ballysadare	26
45	Sligo	Ballysadare	Dromore West	30
46	Sligo	Dromore West	Ballina	33
47	Mayo	Ballina	Rathlachan	37
48	Mayo	Rathlachan	Belderrig	47
49	Mayo	Belderrig	Annie Brady Bridge	50
50	Mayo	Annie Brady Bridge	Belmullet Town	56
51	Mayo	Clogher, Mullet	Ballyglass, Mullet	58
52	Mayo	Ballyglass, Mullet	Tra Bheal, Mullet	61
53	Mayo	Tra Bheal, Mullet	Tra Deirbhile, Mullet	65
54	Mayo	Tra Deirbhile, Mullet	Clogher, Mullet	70
55	Mayo	Belmullet Town	Gaoth Saile	73
56	Mayo	Gaoth Saile	Bangor Erris	77
57	Mayo	Bangor Erris	Ballycroy	81
58	Mayo	Ballycroy	Achill Sound	91
59	Mayo	Achill Sound	Mulranny	96
60	Mayo	Achill Sound	Doogort, Achill	99
61	Mayo	Doogort, Achill	Keel, Achill	101
62	Mayo	Keel, Achill	Achill Sound	110
63	Mayo	Mullranny	Newport	114

64	Mayo	Newport	Rosmoney Pier	117
65	Mayo	Rosmoney Pier	Westport	119
66	Mayo	Westport	Louisburgh	121
67	Mayo	Louisburgh	Louisburgh (loop)	125
68	Mayo	Louisburgh	Leenane	130
69	Galway	Leenane	Tully Cross	135
70	Galway	Tully Cross	Cleggan	140
71	Galway	Cleggan	Clifden	147
72	Galway	Clifden	Ballyconneely	154
73	Galway	Ballyconneely	Peninsula loop	159
74	Galway	Ballyconneely	Roundstone	162
75	Galway	Roundstone	Glynsk	165
76	Galway	Glynsk	Cill Chiarain	172
77	Galway	Cill Chiarain	Rosmuc	182
78	Galway	Rosmuc Peninsula loop		186
79	Galway	Rosmuc	Beal an Daingin	192
80	Galway	Beal an Daingin	Leitir Mor	198
81	Galway	Gorumna Island		202
82	Galway	Leitir Mullan Island		208
83	Galway	Beal an Daingin	Casla	213
84	Galway	Casla (Costello)	Spiddal	222
85	Galway	Spiddal	Salthill	230
86	Galway	Salthill	Oranmore	235
87	Galway	Oranmore	Clarinbridge	250
88	Galway	Clarinbridge	Kinvara	255
89	Galway	Kinvara	New Quay	261

Coasting around Connacht

"I remember vividly a moment as a child when I stood barefoot on firm dry sand by the sea. The sound of breakers on the shore shut out all others. In this supreme moment I leapt in sheer joy and started to run. I glanced around uneasily to see if anyone was watching. A fresh rhythm entered my body. I had found a new source of power - a source I never dreamt existed"
(Roger Bannister from his autobiography, Twin Tracks)

I've often thought of Roger Bannister standing there alone on the beach. I understand how he felt as a young kid with only the sound of the waves crashing on the shore. In the West of Ireland, we are lucky to have so many spectacular beaches to run on. I think our Atlantic coast inspired me too and gives me *'the source of power'* he refers to. Thinking of Bannister running barefoot on the beach also reminds me of the Greeks. They were the original Olympians who insisted that *'sand was for the feet of the runner'*. I love that phrase and those words have followed me around the western shoreline, just as they inspired me on my Ulster coastal run.

Welcome to my continuing story, or my adventure as I like to call it. This journey has been tough but not as difficult as I thought. The secret, like everything in life, is to do it one step at a time, or one kilometre at a time. It's not always smooth running on long sandy beaches. During my journey there were fields to trample through and lots of barbed wire fences to climb over. Every stage I've completed brought its own unique challenge. No matter how much I prepared and planned there was always some obstacle to overcome on the day. After I completed the coast of Ulster (all 1,590 km) I had a vague idea that I would continue along the west coast to my native city of Galway. I'm so glad I persevered as I discovered many new places in Connacht that I hadn't even read about before.

At times I realised that I was running along shorelines that had not been visited in years. I was aware of how *'An Gorta Mor'* (the great famine) and subsequent emigration had decimated areas in the West. I noticed this especially in Connemara and in parts of Mayo. The pre-famine population of Connacht, according to the 1841 census, was **1.42** million. However, one hundred and fifty years later the province had lost exactly one million of its citizens. The 1991 census showed the Connacht population was only 420,000. However, in that same 150-year period (between 1841 and 1991) European economies were thriving. The Netherlands increased its population from 3 million to 15 million (a 400% increase) and England increased theirs from 15 million to 54 million. Rural areas have never really recovered from this loss of its people. Even the latest census of 2022 shows Connacht's population of 590,000, still 800,000 short of the 1841 figure. As I was running along the west coast, I could almost imagine what the pre-famine countryside was like. Some of these remote places have changed very little in two hundred years. Perhaps there is even a lonely feeling about the west coast. Today in Connacht, most people either live in larger towns or in bigger houses in the countryside. I can imagine in pre-famine times hundreds of adults and children wandering through the countryside. On two or three occasions in Connemara I knew that I was running along a path that few had trampled on since the famine. In the Rosmuc peninsula in Connemara I saw a half-completed causeway at *'Snamh Bo'* where, as the name suggests, cows used to swim across. Just a few days later going from '*Muiceanach idir Dhá Sháile*' to *Beal an Daingin* I ran along a boggy trail with a series of unfinished causeways across sea inlets. Why build a road that may never be used because so many have perished, and even more are leaving the area? Sadly, even today some of these rocky causeways and roads are still left in this same unfinished state.

The original Coastal Running Team

Sometimes you just have to do things on your own. I've now completed over 70% of this coastal run entirely alone. Having said that, it was always easier when others joined me or even gave encouragement along the way. When I originally started this journey in February 2017, I was lucky to have found the two perfect partners. You might remember Helen Byers and Sean Nickell from my first book, who were my running buddies. Without them I doubt if I would have ever started this whole adventure. Together the three of us ran around the whole coast of Northern Ireland (all 659km). Admittedly after they left me on my own, I had to run around Donegal (another 931km) and Connacht (another 1,745km). On a few occasions Helen and Sean did come back to join me. They returned to run with me in Donegal (Stage 34) when we crossed over *'One Man's Pass'* at the cliffs of Slieve League. They were with me in Co. Mayo when we climbed Croagh Patrick on St. Patrick's Day in 2022. Then I was so delighted that I was able to show off my native city in July 2023 when we ran through the streets of Galway together.

In fairness they have been busy with their own range of activities. Helen completed another four marathons in 2023. After running the most famous and original in Boston in a time of 3.26 she completed the London Marathon six days later in 3.40. She improved that time in Berlin with her 3.23 and rounded it off with another great run of 3.28 in Dublin. Meanwhile Sean has been doing a few long runs of his own. In September 2023 he tackled the famous 170km Ultra-Trail du Mont-Blanc (UTMB). This run through the Alps has a total elevation of over 9,000 meters (higher than Everest!). Qualifying for this event is an achievement and tens of thousands of runners apply to run. Those lucky enough to qualify assemble in Chamonix at the intersection of the three Alpine countries, France, Italy, and Switzerland. Almost 40% of those who started the race in 2023 did not finish. The cut-off time of 44 hours is difficult to beat but Sean was comfortably under this in a time of 40 hours. I have no doubt that Helen and Sean will return to join me again on the Munster stage of my journey. Also, I'd like to thank two other friends from North Down AC, Donald Smith, and Johnny McGrath. Johnny ran with me in Co. Sligo and Donald joined me once in Co. Mayo and then again in south Connemara.

This caricature of Helen, Sean and I appeared in the local newspaper, the Co. Down Spectator

Recording the coastal run

Logging my adventures and seeing the wee map that traces every stage gives me great satisfaction. The Strava maps also act like a check that I've completed all sections of the coast. It keeps the fictious *'Coastal Audit Committee'* happy too! This book you are now reading is a download of my blog which goes into more detail about every run. I always try to write my blog to help any runner (walker or cyclist) who is trying to tackle any section of the Irish coast.

https://cliftoncoastalrun.blogspot.com/

Clifton School and Rosedale School

This adventure was originally named *'Clifton Coastal Run'* after Clifton Special School in Bangor, Co. Down. My son Brian attended Clifton (a school for children with 'severe learning difficulties') for fourteen years until June 2023. I've already raised £3,688 for Clifton School. As Brian is now nineteen and has left school, I decided to contact a similar special school in Galway, my native city. I messaged Rosedale School and made a connection with parents from that school. Therefore, ALL profits from this book will go to Rosedale Special School.

In March 2024 Brian was twenty years old. Unfortunately, over the last five or six years he has started getting seizures. It's hard to predict when he will next get one of these fits. Our hearts go out to poor Brian going through these convulsions and not been able to do anything about it.

On the positive side, Brian is quite fit and has no physical issues. He has joined me (walking) on a few of my coastal adventures. During our visit to Mayo in August 2021 Brian even climbed to the top of Nephin Mountain. Nephin is higher than Croagh Patrick and is Ireland's tallest stand-alone mountain at 806 meters. After that performance I decided to enroll Brian in our local *'Couch to 5k'* course. This was organized by my athletic club, North Down AC and run by Gordan Matchett and his excellent team. It was a ten-week course and Brian seemed to be making good progress. However, on the ninth week the pressure of running got too much for Brian and he suffered a seizure. Lucky it was a warm and dry evening. We did return the following week to complete the ten-week course, keeping a careful watch on him. Brian still 'graduated' to a 5k with all the others from the course and completed the Bangor parkrun. We were so proud of him.

How long is the coast of Ireland?

I still can't answer this question and it might be a few more years before I can give an accurate reply. I seem to be on track with the Neilson/Costello Trinity Study that calculated the exact distance around every coastal county. You can see from the comparison chart how close I am to their distances, only about 300km or 8% above their calculations. In a 1999 study, Brigitte Neilson and Mark Costello from Trinity College, Dublin measured the whole coast of Ireland as 5,874 km long. I've rounded it up to 6,500 km (4,039 miles), so I'm about halfway there at this stage. The writer Tim Robinson, who walked around the coast of the Connemara, argued that the ***'length of a coastline increases, as if it would never stop, the closer it is investigated'***. He then goes on to refer to a mathematician, Mandelbrot, who wrote a whole paper to answer the question ***'How long is the coast of Britain'***. Personally, I do my best to stick to the coast but if it gets too tricky or dangerous, I will try to look for an alternative inner path or road. I've trampled through fields, bogs and circled tidal islands doing my best to keep strictly to the shoreline. Before my runs, I research a lot on OS maps and Google maps, always trying to find some kind of road or trail that brings me as close to the coast as possible.

GERRY O'BOYLE

Running along the coast of Mayo

Coastal Length: My Run V Neilson/Costello calculation

		Rosedale & Clifton **Coastal Run** <u>Kms</u>	Neilson& Costello <u>Kms</u>
Down		**361**	307
Antrim		**200**	175
Derry		**97**	75
Donegal		**932**	938
Leitrim		**5**	5
Sligo		**227**	211
Mayo		**785**	729
Galway		**728**	642
Covered SO FAR – km		**3,335km**	3,082km
Clare	Estimate	306	306
Limerick *	Estimate	75 *	* 25
Kerry	Estimate	727	727
Cork	Estimate	935	935
Waterford	Estimate	183	183
Kilkenny	Estimate	24	24
Wexford	Estimate	253	253
Wicklow	Estimate	64	64
Dublin	Estimate	155	155
Meath	Estimate	17	17
Louth	Estimate	103	103
Total distance in kms		**6,177km**	5,874km

As I am already a few hundred kilometres above the Neilson/Costello estimate, I reckon that my final mileage around the Irish coast could be about 6,500km or around 4,000 miles. *Also, there is an obvious error in the Neilson/Costello estimate for Co. Limerick. It should be at least 75km.

Hazardous Animals

I thought dogs would be my worst enemy while running along the coast but so far, I've been lucky with our canine friends. Once a black labrador stopped me in my tracks in Donegal and wouldn't let me pass and I had to make a detour. In fairness I think the animal was protecting a young child in a garden. On Conor's Island in Co. Sligo, I was trying to sneak past some horses in an adjoining field, but one of them spotted me and they all gave chase. This was quite scary. I just about won the race back to Streedagh beach beating four or five young thoroughbreds. Another time in Achill, my son Matthew and I were confronted by some sheep. We were in a very remote area when this ram obviously did not like us invading his territory. He faced us aggressively and seemed to be getting into an attacking mode. Unfortunately, we were making our way along a cliff at the time, so we had to be careful with our detour. However, cows have become my least favourite animals. I just don't like them anymore. I hate the way they stare at you. I have never been attacked by a bull …. yet, but on a few occasions, cows have come running towards me. It only seems to take one or two to notice me and the whole herd follow. I worry that I will be a victim of one of those stampedes that you see in a cowboy western. I've now learned to take a wide berth when I see any cattle. On a positive note, I was indebted to the farmer I got chatting to on Omey Island in Connemara. He was herding cows at the time and assured me that his cattle were very friendly. Another reason why Omey is probably my favorite island.

The Irish Coastal Path

Having run around the coast of Ulster and Connacht, I think I'm sufficiently qualified to give my opinion about our coastal path and access to it. At present almost every piece of land in Ireland (North and South) is owned by someone, so in private possession. Permission must be granted by the landowner and that consent could be taken back at any time. The laws are different on the other side of the Irish Sea. In Scotland and England walkers and runners have 'rights to roam' but there are no such rights on the island of Ireland.

I've had a few occasions where I've had to re-route because it was made very clear I was on someone's land. Once on approaching Marble Hill beach in Donegal from the south side

I suddenly came across *'private property'* signs. I struggled along a narrow cliff path with barbed wire making my task quite dangerous. What is this obsession with barbed wire? I've had to climb through so many of these fences on my coastal runs. Even in Northern Ireland I was disappointed that there was not a proper coastal path between Fairhead and Ballycastle. There I saw more 'private property' signs. The only other time I was stopped from running along the coast was in Co. Mayo, in an area known as the *'Lost valley of Uggool'*. I was not surprised on this occasion, as I had read beforehand about the local farmer fencing off his land and his disagreements with hikers. Still, it was a shame that I could not continue my run along this spectacular beach. I know it is spectacular because I did get to see this beautiful area a few weeks later. The owner, Mr. Bourke, organises tours of his land and talks about his family history.

In my opinion the Irish Coastal Path hardly exists at all, well not in Donegal or Connacht. I could easily list the places around the coast that have some kind of path. Nevertheless, there are a lot of quiet country roads on our shores, with very little traffic. The problem with the Irish coastal path is that it is so inconsistent and there is very little signage or information informing what lies ahead. I have come across neglected paths on my journey too. Trails have become overgrown as so few people use them. Once or twice in remote locations in Connemara, I did follow paths on the coast and wondered were these old pre-famine trails created when more people were living in the area. After all my criticism of our Irish coastal path I do enjoy the whole planning and excitement of trying to maneuver my way along the shoreline. It can be so exciting not knowing what's around the next corner. That's what adventures are all about!

Practicalities of running the coast

Sometimes it can be awkward trying to get back to the start after finishing my run. When Helen and Sean were with me in Northern Ireland it was just a matter of taking two cars and leaving one at the finish point. Running on my own proved more difficult. There isn't really a great public transport system in the West of Ireland. That said, I was able to rely on buses on a few occasions in parts of north Donegal, Sligo and in south Connemara. Other times if I was running along a peninsula or tidal island, I was able to loop around and start and finish at the same spot. However, most of the time I relied on the kindness of my wife Maureen to meet me at my finishing point. She has been so supportive and patient with me on this mad adventure. I try to do my best by getting my running done as early as possible. One morning in NW Mayo I got up at 5.00am, had a light breakfast, drove to my starting point, and did a 20km run before returning to our B&B in

Belmullet at 8.00am. I was in time to join Maureen and Brian for a bigger breakfast and then ran another 14km before lunch. Whenever we stayed in a guesthouse, I got into the habit of explaining to the landlady that I would wake early and make my own light breakfast and try to start my run. This meant Maureen and Brian could take their time in the morning before driving to meet me.

I don't mind an early start. There is something magical about getting up at the crack of dawn on a bright June morning to begin a run. Reminds me of one of my favourite books *'As I Walked Out One Midsummer Morning'* by Laurie Lee. His story has probably inspired me on this adventure more than anything I've ever read. I love Laurie's attitude as he leaves his home for the first time. It's 1934 and a sunny morning in Stroud, Gloucestershire.

> *"I was nineteen years old, still soft at the edges, but with a confident belief in good fortune. I carried a small rolled-up tent, a violin in a blanket, a change of clothes, a tin of treacle biscuits, and some cheese."*

He was travelling to London, which was about 160km away, but he choose to make his journey twice as long by heading for the south coast. Laurie had never seen the sea, so he decided to walk to the shore and find it. I always admired him for taking the coastal route, and perhaps unconsciously this encouraged me to tackle a similar journey. Often on my runs, I feel like a nineteen-year-old Laurie Lee, still *'soft at the edges'*. Sometimes you need to embrace this youthful innocence to enhance the whole experience. It's beautiful to read Lee's description of the West Country. It was a different England in the 1930's with little traffic and long before any motorways were built.

> *"Many of the country roads still followed their original tracks, hugging the curve of a valley, or yielding to a promontory like the wandering line of a stream."*

That England of young Laurie Lee (and Thomas Hardy before him) has completely disappeared. We can count ourselves lucky on this side of the Irish Sea. A lot of our roads in Connemara and Mayo still follow their original tracks and *'hug the curve of a valley'*. Some of our countryside has remained unchanged for centuries. Despite my comments earlier about a desolate and lonely Connemara perhaps we should appreciate what we still have.

Near Beal an Daingin, Connemara

The islands of Connacht

- Coney Island, Co. Sligo: Maureen, Brian and I walked across to this island in our bare feet on a beautiful September morning (Stage 44)

- Bartragh Island, Co. Mayo: Sean Harte and gang joined Maureen, Brian, and I on a lovely September afternoon (Stage 47)

- Rosbarnagh Island, Mullet Peninsula: Maureen, Brian and I walked around this small island in July (Stage 51)

- Claggan Island, Co. Mayo: I ran out to this island along a sandbank and met a lovely father and son on their farm. They showed me where the children's burial ground was (Stage 55)

- Inis Bigil, Co. Mayo: This was probably the most difficult island to reach, without getting on a boat. First, I had to cross to Annagh Island at low tide, run about a mile through that island and then run across a long strand to Inis Bigil. (Stage 57)

- Annagh Island, Co. Mayo: Maureen and Brian waited with me for about an hour until the tide was low enough for me to wade across. (Stage 57)

- Inishnakillew, Clew Bay: We crossed a causeway to reach this island and then had beautiful views of the drumlins from a hill we climbed. (Stage 65)

- Inishcottle, Clew Bay: I was able to get here from Inishnakillew Island (Stage 65)

- Achill Island: Officially Ireland's biggest island and there's a bridge linking it to the mainland. This was tough going and hard to avoid the cliffs and hills around the coast (Stages 61 and 62)

- Goreen Island, North Connemara: At low tide I took a shortcut across the bay and was able to reach this island. (Stage 71)

- Omey Island, North Connemara: My favourite island and I had the perfect weather when I circled it. (Stage 71)

- Inis Nee, North Connemara: A chain of three islands. Enjoyed the coastal path on the middle section. (Stage 75)

- Mweenish, South Connemara. Galway: A very soft wet day when I visited in October. (Stage 76)

- Roisin na Chalaidh: South Connemara: It was a miserable day when I was here, and I wasn't too impressed. (Stage 76)

- Finis Island: South Connemara: A beautiful island but only a very short opportunity to cross at low tide. (Stage 76)
- Oilean Mor, Rosmuc: Was able to run along a trail that ran through the island (Stage 78)
- An tOilean Iarthach, Rosmuc: I had to cross Oilean Mor and then a very rocky (and slippery) causeway to reach this island. (Stage 78)
- Eanach Mheain, South Connemara: The rain was coming down as I arrived here. (Stage 80)
- Laidhean Island, South Connemara: This tiny island is reached from Eanach Mheain and there is a golf course here. Nobody was on the greens when I was there in February (Stage 80)
- Leitir Mor, South Connemara: It was just about possible to circle this large island although I had to rough it on the NW side. (Stage 80)
- Gorumna Island, South Connemara: The biggest island of the 'Ceantar Na Oilean' group of islands. It took me a whole morning to circle it (Stage 81)
- Leitir Meallain, South Connemara: Despite its remoteness there seems to be a lot going on. I had lovely tea & scones here at the visitor centre. (Stage 82)
- An Crapach, South Connemara: I didn't stay too long as it seemed to be in private ownership and cows were staring at me. (Stage 82)
- Foirnis Island: South Connemara: I had to cross four causeways to reach it (Stage 82)
- Rosroe Island, Carraroe: I crossed over to this island after doing 'The darkness into Light' walk in Carraroe (Stage 83)
- Hare Island, Galway City: It didn't take me long to circle this wee island in Renmore (Stage 86)
- Tawin Island, Oranmore: Helen & Sean joined me as we ran through some heavy showers (Stage 87)
- Island Eddy, South Galway: It's only accessible at a very low tide so got a guided tour (Stage 89)
- Aughinish Island: This is a unique island as it is strictly in Co. Clare, but you have to cross a causeway from Co. Galway to reach it. Therefore, it's not connected to the rest of Co. Clare. (Stage 89)

Map of Connacht

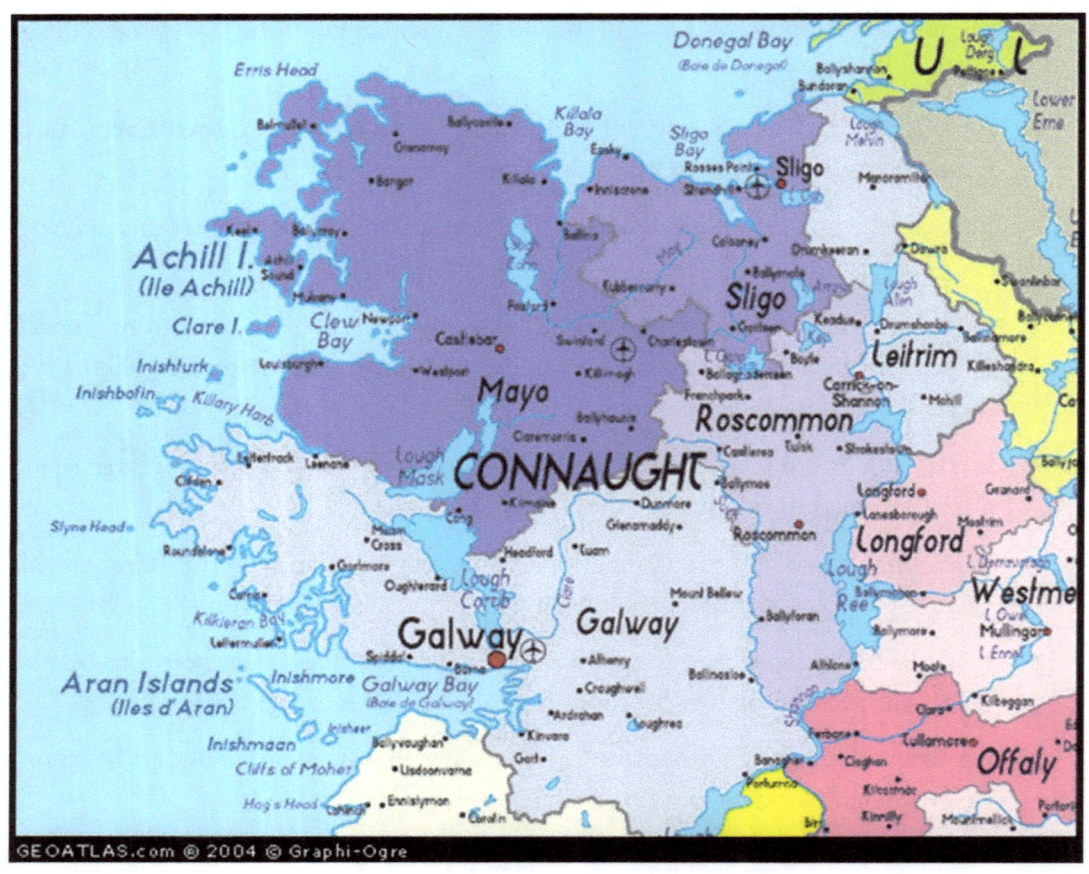

STAGE 41

(or Stage 1 of Connacht section)

Bundoran, Co. Donegal to Grange, Co. Sligo

Saturday 1 February 2020

27.0 km or 16.8 miles

"I've a fine felt hat and a strong pair of brogues – and I'm well prepared to ramble, I must go" from the song, 'Rambles of Spring' by Tommy Makem

Today is 1st February, the start of spring (well, in the Irish calendar anyway). It was great to have my friend Johnny McGrath join me as we crossed into the province of Connacht. It was an early start, leaving Bangor at 6.15am and driving across the counties of Antrim and Tyrone. At Kesh, Co. Fermanagh we took a left turn that took us through Boa Island on Lough Erne and reached the border with the Republic of Ireland just outside Belleek. We drove directly to Grange, Co. Sligo and parked our car outside Moran's Pub, which is today's finish point.

From Bundoran, Johnny and I take an inner coastal route and avoid the busier main road. At Tullaghan we were still able to stay on this Carbery coast road. By the time we came back on the N15 again we had covered the whole coast of Leitrim which didn't take long. After crossing into Co. Sligo, we took the next turn into Grellagh

We're flying through these counties now_it helps that Leitrim's coastline is only 5km

At a caravan park, we took a right turn down a trail which brought us back down to the coast. We had to rough it over rocks for about a half a mile but soon we were on Bunduff Strand which took us right into the beautiful, secluded village of Mullaghmore. This beach is known by experts as one of the best wave surfing spots in the world.

Monday 27 August 1979

Ironically, I also referred to this dreadful day when I started my very first Coastal Run three years ago in Omeath, Co. Louth and ran through Warrenpoint. Back in 1979, the IRA planted two huge bombs and killed 18 soldiers in the Co. Down town. On that same day, just a few hours earlier, the IRA also murdered Lord Mountbatten here in Mullaghmore together with his grandson Nicholas Knatchbull and Nicholas's grandmother, Doreen. A local boy, Paul Maxwell, was also murdered by the IRA in that explosion.

Back in 2020, Johnny and I had promised ourselves a coffee break and so we called into the Quay Bar and enjoyed freshly baked (still warm) scones too. It had been a long morning!

We continued running on the lovely coastal road that looped around Mullaghmore as the sun finally broke through. In front of us stood the majestic Classiebawn Castle, high up on the hill, almost like a scene from a Disney film or even a horror movie. This was of course home to the Mountbatten's until that tragic day in 1979. From here we could also see across to the cliffs of Slieve League in Donegal which I'd run along last July.

Just after the 1km sign to Cliffony we followed a rough trail (at a soccer pitch) down to Trawalua Strand (also called Cliffony Beach). Two things about this beach; it's got dangerous rip tides, and it is one of Ireland's nudist beaches! Clothes or no clothes, though, I'd recommend it!

Stripping off on Nudist Beach

After a while Johnny and I had to leave the beach (rocky section) but there were sand dune paths to run on and lovely views across to Inishmurray Island.

As today was Saint Brigid's Day I had read about a tradition on 1 February in Inishmurray. People carried a figure to represent Brigid and paraded it around bonfires on the island. No sign of any bonfires on Inishmurray but that's not a surprise, as the last inhabitants left there in 1948. Most settled in nearby Moneygold, probably sounded like a prosperous place! 1,500 years ago, Saint Columba came to visit St Molaise on Inishmurray to confess about stealing and copying a manuscript. Molaise had little sympathy for him and as a punishment he banished him from Ireland.

Columba ended up in Scotland and set up a very famous monastery on the island of Iona. That island became the *'Cradle of Christianity'* in Scotland.

It was a beautiful day now, spring-like and I'm sure we heard a curlew celebrating too! As Cliffony strand disappeared, we had to rough it across a field before we reached a farmer's trail which eventually led us back to the main N15 road.

Ben Bulben was getting clearer and bigger now and after a few more miles we finally reached today's destination of Grange.

STAGE 42

Co. Sligo: Grange to Drumcliff

Sunday 2 February 2020

34.4 km or 21.4 miles

"Under bare Ben Bulben's head in Drumcliff churchyard, Yeats is laid. Cast a cold eye on life, on death. Horsemen pass by" WB Yeats own epitaph.

Johnny and I stayed the night in Moran's Bar B&B in Grange, and we woke early to a damp morning. After breakfast, we decided to drive to Drumcliff and run with the sea on our left for a change. As the rain came down, we arrived at today's starting point and parked the car near the church and graveyard where Yeats is buried.

We began running along the coast road towards Carney, veering left at that village and continuing along the country lane until we reached Lissadell House. This was the childhood home of Irish revolutionary, Constance Gore-Booth (Countess Markievicz) who was the first woman to be elected to the House of Commons. Lissadell House was eventually sold in the year 2000 to prominent Dublin barristers, who began to restrict access through the estate. In recent years a group called the *'Lissadell Action Group'* campaigned to have public rights of way through the estate, claiming there had been free access through the estate for the previous hundred years.

When Johnny and I arrived, the gates were closed and in support of the 'Lissadell Action Group' we climbed over the wall and ran through the estate. I knew there was a beach behind the house and soon we were running on the beautiful Lissadell Strand, looking across to Rosses Point and Strandhill. It started to brighten up too - not a bad day for early February.

At the end of Lissadell beach, on the west side, we were still able to follow a grassy path (past the handball alley) but, as often happens on my coastal adventure, the trail ended abruptly. We headed towards Raghly Point. At this stage, Johnny's knee was giving him trouble and he suggested that I do the loop around Raghly on my own and we would meet later at Yellow Strand.

I ran down to Raghly harbour, yet another pier designed by Nimmo, the engineer. Meanwhile Johnny was trying to cross over the headland to Yellow Strand. He returned (as I came back from Raghly) saying it was a big drop down on the other side and in any case, the tide was in too far.

We decided to stick to the country lanes again, sometimes walking and sometimes running. This wasn't a straightforward run today as there were too many country roads to tackle and we never knew which one to take. I was so glad Johnny was with me to navigate. Eventually we came to a junction at Ardtrasna (high crossing) and from here it was a straight run into Grange. Luckily for us Moran's Pub (our finish line!) was just at the T junction as we entered the village.

Stage 42: Revisited: Streedagh Beach and Conor's Island: Saturday 15 February 2020: 14.8km or 9.2 miles

"To all the friends who met me there, with hearts so warm and true.
To each and all, a fond farewell, sweet Dernish Isle, adieu"
(written by an anonymous emigrant from Dernish island, Co. Sligo)

My plan today was to tackle Streedagh beach (near Grange) and run along that long, thin peninsula as far as Dernish Island. I knew that low tide was around 4.00pm so it worked out well as the rain seemed to have died down by then. It had been a mild winter up to now but in the last week there has been two named storms. Storm Ciara bombarded the coast last week and this weekend Storm Dennis was doing his best to cause havoc. I did think about postponing my coastal run but, as it was half-term, it would have been difficult. So, Maureen, Brian and I drove down to Sligo, through the wind, rain, and floods. We arrived at Grange village and drove directly to nearby Streedagh beach and parked our car there. The three of us then began walking along the strand.

Maureen and Brian on Streedagh Strand

We walked together the whole way along the long beach as far as the tiny, Blackrock Island. I then carried on running on my own onto Conor's Island. It's not actually an island anymore but on an 1837 map it was classified as one. Since then, a sandbank has connected it to the mainland. At this stage Maureen and Brian turned back and we arranged to meet later in Moran's pub in Grange.

I pushed on through the sand dunes all the way along Conor's Island until I was very close to Dernish Island across the rocks. It was almost low tide now, but it would have been a real struggle to get through those rocks to reach Dernish. There was no proper causeway to the island, and I reckon it would <u>not</u> have been safe to even attempt to cross. In the distance I could see Classiebawn Castle in Mullaghmore. In fact, the original site for the Castle was on Dernish Island.

I turned around and headed back, looping around on the south side of Conor's Island. In a field in the distance, I spotted about 10 or 12 horses and the animals seem to spot me too. I noticed one or two of the horses starting to head in my direction. I sprinted over the hills almost afraid to look behind as they chased after me. I was so relieved to be back on Streedagh Beach again.

Once I calmed down, I couldn't help reflecting on the historical significance of this area. In 1588 the storms here were so severe that three different ships of the Spanish Armada crashed. The Spanish Navy lost so many vessels along the western coast but here on Streedagh they had their worst experience. Remember, the Spanish were losing the ***'Battle of Gravelines'*** against the British Navy and decided to take the scenic route northeast from the English Channel. The Armada circled around Scotland before trying to navigate along the west coast of Ireland.

After running along Streedagh strand I followed the headland south all the way round, through fields and mud. Storm Dennis seemed to have picked up again and the wild Atlantic was battling away. I eventually made it back onto the road and soon I was enjoying some Cidona and Taytos with Maureen and Brian in Moran's.

Back in Grange in front of Spanish Armada Mural

STAGE 43

Co. Sligo: Drumcliff to Sligo Town

Sunday 16 February 2020

22.6 km or 14.0 miles

We stayed the night in the Clayton Hotel in Sligo town. In the morning, Maureen drove me to Drumcliff village, and we paused at Yeats Grave (casting a cold eye, on life and death).

At Cafe in Drumcliff with a portrait of Yeats in the background

I headed south along the N15 and just after passing through Rathcormack, I took a right turn. I followed the signs for Lower Rosses and eventually I was able to stick to the coast along the long narrow peninsula all the way to the most northern point.

Trying to hold back the wind at Rosses Point with Ben Bulben behind

When I turned around to head back south towards Rosses Point, I faced the full impact of Storm Dennis and the wild Atlantic wind. I was lucky I had my hat and snood to protect me from the sand blowing in from the shore. Soon I reached Rosses Point Golf Course – no mad golfers out today! I kept struggling against the strong wind and to make matters worse, the rain now arrived. However, I could now see the pier at Rosses Point and civilisation.

I was getting wet now, so I walked into the first hostelry I could find in Rosses Point. It was the Yeats County Hotel (YCH). Ordering a coffee and water I headed towards the open fire to warm up and dry out. Here I got talking to some visitors from Armagh and they kindly let me dry some of my clothes by the fire while I drank my coffee. When I was leaving, one of them kindly gave me a donation - thank you Declan McAlinden and friends!

From here it was a straight run into Sligo Town - the sign said 8km - but it was still a tough ending to today's adventure. I continued, eventually crossing the river Garavogue into Sligo town to meet Maureen and Brian.

STAGE 44

Co. Sligo: Sligo Town to Ballysadare

Monday 17 February 2020

31.3km or 19.4 miles

Thankfully Storm Dennis had died down and I only suffered one heavy shower today. Sticking by the coast as always, I followed the dock road in Sligo after I crossed the river. As I came into Strandhill, I was lucky to spot a sign pointing towards the *'Killaspugbrone Loop'*. This was a lovely path that led me down to the shore and took me past Sligo Airport.

I followed the coast all the way around and came to the ancient Killaspugbrone church and graveyard that St. Patrick once visited. After leaving the old churchyard I was still able to follow a grassy path to the tip of the peninsula and loop around back towards the village of Strandhill.

Meeting Brian in Strandhill, Co. Sligo

Shortly Maureen and Brian arrived, and we enjoyed some coffee and scones in Shells Cafe. Soon I was running again – this time, south towards the sand dunes. As it was high tide there was no possibility to run on the beach. In any case, running through the dunes was an interesting experience and took me around the bottom of Strandhill peninsula. I then came to Culleenamore beach. Not really sand for the feet of the runner, as it was much too soft. At least the weather has brightened up.

Leaving Culleenamore strand I took a right turn towards Ballysadare, following the R292 for a few miles with Knocknarea (Queen Maeve's grave) on my left. At this stage I was struggling – running three days in a row was taking its toll – so I decided to walk the hills. Still, nobody said this adventure was going to be easy – and soon I had reached Ballysadare, my destination for this weekend.

Stage 44: Revisited: Co. Sligo's Coney Island: Sunday 20 September 2020 13.1km or 8.1 miles

I knew that I needed a low tide to be able to run (or walk) across to Coney Island and we got the perfect day to do this. I had completed Stage 48 in NW Mayo the day before and I was so glad that Maureen and Brian could join me today on a less strenuous adventure. Coney Island is sometimes called Inishmulclohy.

Getting ready to walk to Coney Island

Coney or ***coinín*** is really the Irish word for rabbit. Apparently, the New York Coney Island is called after this one as the sea-captain of a ship called the 'Arethusa' (that used to sail between Sligo and New York) noticed lots of rabbits on the New York Island and it reminded him of Sligo's Coney Island.

It's a good 2.5km across to the island from the mainland and we had the most beautiful day with Ben Bulben watching over us the whole time. There are 14 (rock) markers about 150 metres a part to guide you on the way to the island.

On reaching Coney I put my running shoes back on, left Maureen and Brian, and ran clockwise (sea on my left) around the island. Eventually I arrived at Carty's Strand on the west side of the island where I had arranged to meet Maureen and Brian again.

We still had plenty of time on the island and we were even able to stop at Wards pub for some coffee (and crisps for Brian) before walking slowly across the strand back to the mainland. It was such a lovely day that will forever live in my memory. Bye, bye Coney Island.

STAGE 45

❖

Co. Sligo: Ballysadare to Dromore West

Saturday 14 March 2020

40.3 km or 25.0 miles

'She bid me take love easy, as the leaves grow on the tree;
But I, being young and foolish, with her would not agree'.
Salley Gardens by WB Yeats

I'm travelling on my own this weekend as we were worried about taking Brian away, especially in these worrying times of Coronavirus. I drove down on the Friday evening, staying two nights in the lovely 'Twin Trees' hotel in Ballina. With all that is going on in the world there is an eerie atmosphere in the hotel, and I even spotted one guest wearing a face mask.

I started my run in Ballysadare or **_Baile Easa Dara_** (town of the waterfall of the oak) where the song 'Salley Gardens' originated. You could say WB Yeats co-wrote it. He said it was an *'attempt to reconstruct a song that he heard an old peasant lady singing'*

I was lucky that I was able to depend on public transport this weekend as I was travelling between Connacht's second largest town (Sligo) and its fourth largest (Ballina).

Ballysadare was originally a major gathering place for all surrounding districts. Saint Columba visited here in 575 AD *'where all the prelates of the neighbouring regions, and vast numbers of holy men and women had come to meet him'.* 'Also, another famous saint, Féichín was born in the townland of Billa in the parish of Ballysadare.

Leaving Ballysadare I ran along the main Ballina Road for about 2km until I came to the sign for Streamstown. This was a quiet country road with Ben Bulben still visible in the distance and as the boreen looped around again, the Ox mountains (or Slieve Gamph) became visible. I think it's an exaggeration referring to these wee hills as mountains. I arrived back onto the main road again and soon came to the village of Beltra.

View from Streamstown with Ben Bulben behind

About one kilometre after Beltra, I took another right, signposted *'Coast Road'*. No discussion about taking this turn! I followed this road for about 2km towards Portavaud down to the shore. Here I spotted a man on crutches coming out of the water with seaweed over his legs. I got talking to him (Rodney) and he explained that he had a biking accident and heard that seaweed was a good remedy.

The weather now turned wet and miserable as I circled Portavaud Point at the end of the peninsula. Lots of sheep in this area and all protecting their young, newborn lambs. Shortly I saw the sign for Dunmoran Strand. When I arrived on the beach I was soaked to the skin, and I hesitated as I wasn't sure if I could continue along the shore all the way to Aughris. I debated with myself whether I'd be better following a country road inland instead. In the end I decided to risk it on the beach, and it paid off. I was probably lucky that the tide was half-way out.

It was a rocky shore but soon I got through it, and I was well rewarded as there was a pub called the Beach Bar at the end. I decided to call in and had a nice pot of tea while my clothes dried by the fire. However, I was surprised there were so many people in the pub with all the warnings about Coronavirus. I got to talk to a couple of guys in the pub asking them for directions to Easkey and Dromore West. They assured me I'd reach my destination in 'no time at all'. I'm always amazed in these situations how non-runners in a pub can overestimate how fast you can run.

After leaving the bar, the rain came down again. I soldiered on, following the coast road towards Easkey and Dromore West. I knew the Ballina-Sligo bus only ran every two hours so I was trying to make sure I would get the 2.45 from Dromore West.

At the bus stop in Dromore I called into a café and ordered a coffee. I had barely got my drink when the bus arrived to take me back to Ballysadare. Luckily, I had spare clothes in my car. It was probably my wettest coastal run since crossing the Foyle Bridge in Derry at the end of Stage 15 back in March 2018.

STAGE 46

Dromore West, Co. Sligo to Ballina, Co. Mayo

Sunday 15 March 2020

48.4 km or 30.1 miles

Thankfully it was a much nicer day today. I decided it would be more practical to run clockwise, with the sea on my left-hand side and then get the bus back to Ballina from Dromore West. I am totally dependent on public transport this weekend. Before I left Ballina, I got to talk to Rachel, the Manager of Twin Trees Hotel where I stayed, and she kindly donated to my cause. I really appreciated that, as the following day all hotels in the country were closed due to government restrictions on Coronavirus.

Leaving Ballina, I followed the River Moy all the way towards the sea. Years ago, I remembered visiting Ballina and going to a pub along the river to hear jazz music on a Sunday morning.

When I reached Enniscrone, I took a left turn across a field at the Pig' statute and the Diamond Coast Hotel, and then ran along a stream and circled the whole golf course face. Eventually I got down onto the beach from the golf course and ran along this strand for miles, with Bartragh Island now so close on my left. I passed the seaweed baths and continued along a road and trail after that. However, as often happens on my coastal adventure, the trail abruptly ended. I decided to rough it along here, crossing through fields and climbing under (and over) electric fences! I did eventually find a country lane that brought me back onto the R297 road.

After passing Leaffoney School, I took a left turn at the L6409 by the Cabragh River. I followed this road down towards the coast towards Pullaheeney Harbour. When I reached the pier, I expected to be able to continue along the coast as it looked on the Ordnance map. However there didn't seem to be any road north of the harbour. It turned out that some sand and rocks from the sea had covered it over the years. Obviously, clearing the stones has become a losing battle against the Atlantic Ocean.

The road taken by the power of the ocean

I carried on running over the rocks and after about 1km, the road gradually reappeared again. When it eventually turned inland, I ran down towards the coast. There was no path along the shore but there was a lower cliff shelf that I was able to run on. I carried on, reaching the headland at Lenadoon Point.

With all talk about the Coronavirus, the term *'self-isolation'* is being used a lot now. No danger of me catching any virus as I was completely on my own along this part of the Atlantic coast. I think it was at a place called Brownstown where the Finned River flows into the sea that I eventually left the coast.

Arriving in Easkey (which literally means 'plenty of fish')

I stopped briefly in Easkey to refuel but I was conscious that I needed to be in Dromore West to make the 3.50 pm bus back to Ballina. I took a left turn signposted to Easkey Beach and followed the coast road for a while and then came back onto the R297 again.

I just made it to Dromore West on time and was one of only two passengers on the bus to Ballina. With talk of staying indoors and lockdowns on the news it's hard to know when exactly my next coastal run will take place, but I'm determined that the adventure <u>will</u> continue.

STAGE 47

Co. Mayo: Ballina to Kilcummin Strand

Saturday 22 August 2020

41.2km or 25.6 miles

"The French are in Killala, the hour is now at hand, for which we've sighed and waited and prayed for fervently" (Lays of South Sligo, John O'Dowd 1889)

It's good to be back! I did wonder when exactly my Coastal Run would continue. Remember, I had just got Stage 46 completed on 15 March before everything shutdown because of the Coronavirus. Now I've reached Co. Mayo, the county with a notorious long coastline.

At least *'Storm Ellen'* which has been battling our shores has eased off. It was just Maureen and I making the long trip to Ballina, staying again at the lovely Twin Trees Hotel in the town. I waited a long time to continue this coastal run and I deliberately picked today (22 August) as I knew it was the exact anniversary of General Humbert's landing at Kilcummin pier (just north of Killala) in 1798.

I did consider dressing exactly like Humbert, wearing *"a long green hunting frock and a huge conical fur cap"* but I don't think I would have been able to run very far in that gear! As it happened, I forgot to pack my shorts and I only noticed this at 9.00pm the night before! I remembered I had a North Down AC tracksuit bottom in the car and after borrowing some scissors from reception I was able to improvise, although Maureen did comment that I cut too much off one leg of the tracksuit!

I had a quick breakfast in our bedroom in Ballina and began my run at exactly 8.00am. Maureen promised to meet me later at the finish line on Lachan Strand at 1.30pm. Low tide was 2.00pm.

I headed north towards Belleek Forest just outside the town. This was a lovely path through the woods and, although it was now raining relentlessly, I was somewhat protected as I ran through the trees. At the end of the forest, I then took a right turn onto Knockatinnole road. It's nicknamed *'Frenchman's Road'* as General Humbert and his men would have marched this way.

I didn't delay in Killala and decided to keep running north and after about 1km I take a right turn signposted *'Ross Strand 3km'*. With all the rain, this country lane is flooding now but I try to avoid the puddles and run all the way down to the beach itself. I get talking to some brave sea water swimmers (called the 'Grim Reapers') who have just been in for a swim. As we're chatting, the rain finally stops, and the sun is even trying to make an appearance. It's just 10.00am.

I leave Ross Beach, run back up the road again and continue in the direction of Ballycastle. After about 3km I cross the river Cloonaghmore at Palmerstown (or Parsonstown) - *'a majestic stone bridge of eleven arches'* as Valerian Gribayedoff called it in 1890.

After crossing Parsonstown bridge, I take the road to the right, heading north along *'Humbert's Way'* and passing *'Rathfran Graveyard'*. I'm able to loop around by the ancient cemetery and then continue along a coastal lane until I get as far as a T junction at Castlemagee.

At this stage I've run about 20 miles, my legs are feeling heavy and I'm walking up the hills. The good news is that the warm August breeze is drying my shirt and shorts. I eventually rejoined Humbert's trail which leads me all the way down to Kilcummin Pier. This is the exact spot where Humbert and his men arrived in 1798.

General Humbert and his men had left La Rochelle in France on 4th August to great crowds that *'shouted themselves hoarse to the army of Ireland'*. There were only 1,130 troops in his 'army' on the three ships. Compare that to the 14,450 French soldiers accompanied by Wolf Tone that tried to land in Bantry, Co. Cork two years earlier but did not disembark due to severe gales. Among the soldiers and officers in Humbert's small army was Wolf Tone's brother, Matthew. Another Irishman with Humbert was his interpreter Henry O'Keon who was born in Kilcummin, and this is probably the main reason why they landed in this part of Mayo. Humbert also brought 5,500 arms for the 'Irish peasantry' who he hoped would join him. He maintained....

"We have come to your country, not as conquerors, but as deliverers"

Standing on 'Humbert's Stone' where his small army landed exactly 222 years ago

Even before Humbert's men arrived in Ballina there were rumours already spreading in the town about the oncoming French army. Letters had been distributed in Ballina looking for Irish volunteers to join Humbert. A young man, Patrick Walsh had been caught with one of these letters the day before Humbert's army arrived, and without any kind of trial he was hanged in the Crane at the Ballina market. Walsh's body was still hanging when Sarrazin (Humbert's second in command) arrived with his men. I am indebted to Valerian Gribayedoff a 19th century writer who in 1890 described the exact scene (illustrating it too) when Sarrazin and Humbert's men arrived in Ballina and spotted Walsh's hanging body at the crane.

'Sarrazin stepped up to the crane, threw his arms around the inanimate form and imprinted a kiss on the livid brow. He then ordered Walsh's body to be cut down, carried to the nearest chapel, and attired in a French military suit. His body was then placed in a handsome coffin and all this to the tune of 'Marseillaise'.

Sarrazin (Humbert's 2nd in command) at Walsh's hanging body

This ritual of respecting Michael Walsh's death and treating him like a martyr impressed the local Irish more than anything else and many joined the French men after this. Humbert's small, but growing army, then went on to trick and deceive General Lake, the British army commander, by taking the road west of Loch Conn to Castlebar. They marched south and won a famous battle in the Mayo town despite being outnumbered by three to one. In defeat General Lake and his men ended up galloping away and so the battle became known as **'The Races of Castlebar'**. Humbert then declared **'A Republic of**

Connacht' but of course like all Irish uprisings, it eventually ended in tears. For General Humbert and his men, defeat came a few weeks later in Co. Longford.

Back in the year 2020 the weather was brightening up nicely for me. I left Kilcummin Pier and headed north once again. As I walked up a steep trail (which was my final hill of the day) I stopped to chat to a lady. I told her I was going to run along Killcummin Strand and cross the river to reach the other side of Rathlachan. She shook her head *'No, you can't cross that river'* and then added that, if I was going to attempt to cross it *'to take a line at the church on the hill and cross at that point'*. She emphasized, not to cross the stream too near the sea as the current would be too strong.

I carried on and as I came to the top of the hill a beautiful view stretched out in front of me. It was Killcummin Strand in all its beauty.

Kilcummin Strand

I ran along the cliff top road and shortly was able to get down onto the beach. I knew it was low tide at 2.00pm too, so everything was going well so far. When I finally got to the end of the long beach, I spotted Maureen in her pink top in the distance. However, as I got closer to her, I noticed that there was a big stream, maybe eight metres wide, between us. The sand was also very soft in this area and there was a slight current on the river. And so, for the next fifteen minutes we both looked for a good crossing point, Maureen on the far side of the river and me on this side. We were like two young lovers trying to communicate across a dangerous border.

I remembered what the lady had said earlier *'take a line at the church'* and as it happened, we were at that exact point. I could see the church on the hill behind Maureen on the other side, but it still looked too risky to cross over the river.

Eventually we decided it was going to be too difficult and so we arranged to meet back on Kilcummin Pier. Maureen was able to drive back to the pier from her side of the river and I had a nice 2km stroll in the afternoon sun, returning along the beach. On the way back I met that same lady again. She said she had heard that years ago women used to cross over to Rathlachan and used the church on the hill as a marker or line. Still, I was glad I didn't risk crossing over. Anyway, being reunited with my wife Maureen on Kilcummin Pier (where Humbert originally landed) was quite a nice romantic ending to today's adventure.

Stage 47 Revisited: Bartragh Island: Saturday 2 September 2023: 14.1km or 8.8 miles

'We are safe here for a while together above the tides reach',
Tony Hegarty's poem about Bartragh.

I saw this island first from Enniscrone beach on the Sligo side (Stage 46) and then later from Ross Strand near Killala (Stage 47). I wasn't sure if it was possible to run (or walk) across and I didn't want to take any risks either. However, if it was achievable, I needed to get there. My dilemma was solved by Denis Quinn from *'Wild Atlantic Cultural Tours'* and we booked a trip across with him.

Our team of SIX for today (with Aoife, Cassandra & Sean)

I was also privileged to have my old friend Sean Harte from Galway with us today. His daughter Aoife and her friend Cassandra Beggan also joined us. I have known Sean and Cassandra's parents for over forty years. I was so pleased that they all came along. Such great company which added to the whole adventure. With Maureen and Brian, we now had a team of six. We arranged to meet our guide Denis, at 1.30pm in Killala and he then drove us a few miles away, to a townland called Ballockpark, which is about 1km south of Moyne Friary. From there we were able to walk across to Bartragh Island. I had told Denis about my Coastal Run, so I left the others for a while and ran ahead to the north side of the island and headed west along the beach.

In my absence, the others visited the only house on the island. It was built by the Kirkwood family in the 1830's. In the 1940's Claud Kirkwood inherited the house. He was a recluse (perfect place he found) and once was referred to in a newspaper article as the loneliest man in the world. On one occasion he placed an advertisement in the local paper saying that the island was closed to visitors ***'Due to the thieving proclivities of certain individuals, Bartragh Island is now closed from this date.'***

Just after the Second World War, Claude sold Bartragh to a man named Captain Verner. Verner's wife was a sister of the actress Joyce Redman, who was nominated for two academy awards. She entertained some Hollywood friends here. *'Gone with the Wind'* actress Vivien Leigh attempted a visit, but the weather did not permit it. Maybe she could have used a guide, like Denis.

In 1978, the whole island was offered for sale for £95,000. Seemed like a good deal as in the early 2000's it was purchased for €1.5million by a consortium led by golfer Nick Faldo. I have seen a video of Faldo talking about a golf course on the island and he seemed very passionate about the whole idea. He loved natural links courses and had even marked out various holes in the sand dunes. However, for some reason the idea for a golf course never developed. As recently as April 2021 the island was sold again for €1million.

Shipwreck - probably SS Sine

While Maureen and the others were visiting Bartragh House, I was making my way along the north shore of the island, running as far west as I could. It was not always *'sand for the feet of the runner'* as I often quote, but most of the time it was a good surface. I passed two shipwrecks quite close to each other on the NW corner of the island. In November 1927 during a storm a Danish ship named the *'SS Sine'*, which was anchored in Killala Bay, was torn free from her moorings. All that is left today of the two wrecks is timber protruding from the sand. I'm not sure if the other one is the *'Lady Washington'*, which apparently crashed near here in 1867.

When I eventually returned to the south-eastern side of the island, I joined the others. I was just in time to see a whole colony of seals relaxing in the sunshine on a sand bank in the bay. Our guide Denis had such a great knowledge of the flora, fauna, and all types of sea creatures. He also knew the exact spots, and underneath which rocks, to find mussels and clams. For the next fifteen minutes we all rummaged in the sand as if nothing else in the world mattered. Even Brian got into the act, spotting some cockles, and digging them up. What a lovely way to spend a beautiful summer's day. Yes, it is September, but today is probably the warmest and sunniest day since June. Still in our bare feet we slowly made our way back to the main shore after a wonderful day's adventure. Later Sean had the privilege of cooking his seafood cocktail or *'Bartragh Island bounty'* as he called it.

Digging for cockles on Bartragh Island

STAGE 48

❖

Co. Mayo: Lachan Strand to Beal Deirg

Saturday 19 September 2020

37.7 km or 23.4 miles

'To lift the lid of the peat and find this pupil dreaming of neolithic wheat.'
(Seamus Heaney wrote this after he met Patrick Caulfield in 1974.
Patrick was the man who discovered the Céide Fields - see later)

Waking to a sunny morning Maureen drove me back (almost) to the point where I finished Stage 47. If you remember, last month I tried to get across the narrow stretch of Lachan Bay but in the end decided it was a little dangerous to try to cross the river. So, I began Stage 48 on the west side of Lachan Strand, running north towards Downpatrick Head. My plan for today was to run to Porturlin (Port Durlainne) but as you will read later, that didn't happen!

Dun Briste at Downpatrick Head

I headed north along the coast road from Rathlachan. After about 8km I spotted the sign for Downpatrick Head. There is a massive and spectacular cliff ledge here that broke off the coast. It is 50 metres high and only 50 metres from the main coastline. It's called

Dun Briste. There was a strong storm here in 1393, which caused the arc or bridge that connected the two parts to collapse overnight. (briste means break in Irish).

Nearby are ruins of a church that was founded by St. Patrick, hence the name Downpatrick. There is also an underground cave (Poll na Seantuinne) on this headland. It was here that thirty local people were drown as they escaped British soldiers in September 1798. This was really a *'revenge act'* after General Humbert's victories in Ballina and Castlebar. See my previous report on Stage 47.

I left Downpatrick Head, running south towards Ballycastle and then crossed a stream on the beach. There's something refreshing about taking your shoes off and dipping your feet in the cool sea water. I'm back on the R314 again along the twisty and hilly coastal road, but I was determined to keep running until I reached the Céide Fields. The discovery of the Fields began in the 1930s when Patrick Caulfield, working in the bog, noticed piles of rocks that must have been placed there before the bog developed. Forty years later Patrick's son, Seamus, having studied archaeology, investigated further, and discovered, under the bog, a system of fields, houses, and megalithic tombs.

Today it's warming up nicely now, but my legs were suffering up those hills. I kept running as far as Belderrig, making sure to take a right turn after the bridge in the village.

I was in no condition to run another 13k to Porturlin, so I decided to call it a day at the pier at Belderrig. Even calling Belderrig a village is a bit of an overstatement - there really is so little here. However, all that could have been so different if there had been a railway line to Belmullet with a station here. This was a seriously considered project at the beginning of the twentieth century and there was even a hotel built in Belderrig in anticipation. So instead of getting a train back to Ballina, Maureen and Brian had to drive to the pier to collect me.

STAGE 49

Co. Mayo: Beal Deirg to Annie Brady Bridge

Saturday 12 June 2021

50 km or 31.1 miles

"But now if anybody says anything about war or even fight, I will just run and run and run" Kenule Beeson, Nigerian writer.

Back again after another long Covid interrupted break. I have a nervous excitement about today's run as it's been nine months since the last one. However, the long delay has given me more time to complete my book (Ulster Coastal Run) which covers the first 40 stages of my Coastal adventure.

Today I'm in a very remote corner of north-west Mayo. It's a general area called Erris. The Irish naturalist, Robert Prager, described this part of Mayo as **'the wildest, loneliest stretch of any county to be found in Ireland'.**

However, he did go on to say, **'I find such a place not lonely or depressing, but inspiring'.**

Readers of the Irish Times voted this Erris region **'the best place to go wild in Ireland'** and I'm tempted to strip off and go a bit wild myself. Maureen, Brian, and I are staying in the Yellow Rose B&B in Belderrig, and our hosts Eileen and Stephen looked after us over the weekend.

I decided on an early start this morning with a light breakfast of Weetabix and banana. Stephen at the B&B even got up and kindly made me tea and toast before I started my run from his house at 6.30am. Maureen and Brian opt for the full Irish breakfast at 9.00am and we arrange to meet later.

I'm feeling confident about my fitness as I've done a few long runs in the last few months in preparation for this weekend. In addition, I completed a 50k (31 miles) race at Down Royal Racecourse just two weeks ago with a time of 4 hours 55 minutes. That involved running seventeen times around the racecourse. In horseracing terms, that is 248 furlongs - at least there were no fences to jump over! I've also recently had my second Covid vaccine so I should be good to go today.

I take the quiet country coastal road (just outside the B&B) from Belderrig to Porturlin. I wondered why Eileen at the B&B called it the *'high road'*, but I quickly found out as I seemed to be climbing for the first couple of miles. In fact, the story of today was all about hills. My Strava results tell me that my total elevation today was 1,818 metres – by far the highest of any stage I've done so far.

It's a 13km run to Porturlin this morning and I have this narrow road to myself, only meeting two vehicles along the way.

Sheep on Porturlin High Road

However, I did have my road blocked by sheep at one stage and there was no room to overtake them. I must have run behind them for a good 2km – the faster I went, the faster they went! I felt particularly sorry for the young lambs trying to keep up with their parents. Eventually I was able to herd the sheep into a gap in a forest and continue my run.

When I arrive at Porturlin (or Port Durlainne) it's still very quiet. There is evidence though that this is a proper fishing port with boats of all sizes here in this wee harbour. Mackerel, herring, salmon, cod and pollock are the main catches here. (Later back at the B&B I was able to enjoy some of this tasty mackerel for dinner).

At the pier I must decide whether to stick to the country roads which would have taken me a few kilometers inland or follow the direct (over the headland) route towards Portacloy. As the weather was still quite dry, I decided to stick to the coast. It was a long steep climb up the hill and as I got higher, I could feel the strong Atlantic wind on my face. The beautiful views back down to Porturlin harbour made it all worthwhile.

I follow the rough grassy headland along the cliff. Sometimes it's like running on a deluxe carpet but at other times I'm sinking into the bogland. I read somewhere that bog is 90% water, and it does feel like that today with *'its soft and craggy boglands'* as the Sawdoctors call it.

The cliffs are spectacular along here and after a lot of hard climbing I can eventually see the secluded Portacloy beach below me. I descend slowly and, on the strand, I stop to chat to a young family who have the whole place to themselves.

Oliw and her family on Portacloy strand

I carry on running on the other side of the beach, climbing again until I see the marked Carrowteige Loop. Just west of the beach I cross over a stile and then there are small wooden markers, every 50 metres or so, all the way around the headland. After leaving Portacloy I took a detour off the path to the top corner of the peninsula and spotted a huge stone EIRE sign on the grass beside the cliff top.

These big *'EIRE signs'* were made of rocks during WW2 so that aircraft flying overhead would know they were entering Ireland, a neutral country. This symbol even has the no. 63 beside it. (There were 83 signs in total all around the coast of Ireland erected during WW2).

I get back onto the Carrowteige Loop and shortly I can clearly see the famous stags of Broadhaven. In my previous coastal run from Killala to Belderrig I spotted these tall sea stacks in the distance, so I was looking forward to getting a much closer look. These five massive rocks rise out of the ocean to about 100 metres above sea level. All the stags have different names. The highest and central one is called Donal O'Cleirigh and one of the tall rocks is bisected by a long narrow cave.

I don't meet anyone else along this Carrowteige loop despite it been a pleasant June morning and a Saturday. I feel like I'm the only person on the planet. Even this dark brown landscape of bogs and cliffs looks slightly lunar!

I had arranged to meet Maureen and Brian on Rinroe strand, near Carrowteige and I was looking forward to a good rest. It's 11.00 am now and I've run about 35km (22 miles) and already climbed 1,700 metres today. This is the perfect place to have a wee break. Rinroe beach along with Portacloy Beach (see earlier) have both been recognised for their *'clean environment, excellent water quality and natural beauty'* and have been awarded a Green Coast Award.

I continue on the beach for a few miles with perfect 'sand for the feet of the runner'. I had earlier checked the tide (low tide was at 2.00pm) which worked out perfect for me as I was able to take a short cut across to Rossport (Ros Dumhach) peninsula.

Rossport and Shell Gas Pipeline

I first heard about Rossport in 2005 when five local men were jailed for refusing to allow the oil company, Shell access to their lands. Shell, with permission from the Irish government proposed to lay a high pressure, raw gas pipeline through the village and insisted that the pipeline was designed to the highest engineering standards and was safe.

However local people disagreed and protested. Five men, known as the *'Rossport Five'* were jailed for 94 days for their refusal to obey a High Court order forbidding them from obstructing Shell's construction of the gas pipeline through their lands. Following a review, and after the men were freed from three months in jail, Shell agreed to re-route the pipe to move it further from the men's land.

Rossport Pier: Shell still not popular in this area

Admittedly Shell didn't have a great history in protecting the environment in other countries. They were criticised for causing pollutions and some alleged human rights violations in Nigeria. Kenule Beeson was a famous Nigerian writer and led a campaign against damage to the environment in Africa. Despite his non-violent campaign (see also his words/quotation at the beginning of Stage 49) he was executed by the military dictatorship in his own country. Meanwhile in Mayo in 2018, Shell exited the project, selling its ownership stake to Vermilion Energy.

After arriving on Rossport Pier, I join a country road and finally reach my finish point at Annie Brady Bridge. Today's mileage was 49.8km so while I'm waiting for Maureen and Brian to come, I run 100 metres further on (and back again) to make it a round 50km.

STAGE 50

Co. Mayo: Annie Brady Bridge to Belmullet town

Sunday 13 June 2021

35.8 km or 22.2 miles

'Time and tide wait for no man' Geoffrey Chaucer

My whole body is suffering today and I'm not as quick to jump out of bed this morning. I enjoy the lovely breakfast that Eileen and Stephen cooked for us at the Yellow Rose B&B. After we check out Maureen and Brian drive me back to the Brady Bridge to start today's run. There are not many towns or villages around here, so it seemed a good idea to pick this bridge over the Muingnabo (mane of the cow) river, as a finish line yesterday and starting point today. Yesterday as I waited on the bridge for Maureen and Brian, a man stopped his tractor to see if I was ok. ***'I thought you were going to jump in the river'***, he said.

History of Annie Brady Bridge

During the Great Famine and before the bridge was built, this river crossing became a well-known, but sad parting point between the emigrants and their remaining families. Annie Brady was the wife of the Inspector of Fisheries for the area and noticed these sad scenes. She decided to raise money to build a bridge at the site to help people to travel further with their loved ones.

At 10.50am I start today's run from the bridge. Yesterday's exploits are taking their toll and I'm wondering will I make it all the way to Belmullet. I reach the main road and follow it for about a mile before taking a right turn towards Pullathomas (Pholla a tSomais).

At Pullathomas (yes sounds like a famous children's tank engine!), there is a hostel and a pub. However, with Covid restrictions still in place both establishments are closed and there is absolutely nobody about today. My legs are moving better now and I'm pleasantly surprised that I can do any running at all today after yesterday's exploits. I struggled on the last few miles into Belmullet (in Irish, it's called Beal an Mhuirthead). I was so glad to see Maureen and Brian there to greet me at the pier in the town.

STAGE 51

Co. Mayo: Mullet Peninsula: Clogher to Ballyglass Lighthouse

Saturday 10 July 2021

46.3 km or 28.8 miles

'A peninsula is an island, hedging its bets, a place of uncertainty, given neither to land or sea' Dermot Healy from 'A Goat's Song'

Last night Maureen, Brian and I stayed in Clogher on the Mullet peninsula, in a lovely B&B called *'Bru Chlann Lir'*. Our host Josephine entertained us over the four or five days.

Road to beach near our B&B

It was the perfect morning as I left the B&B at 6.30am, heading east to a nearby beach, Tra Fheorainn (or Tra Mullach Rua) and then north when I reached the strand. After coasting around Elly Bay, I took a right towards Rosbarnagh Island.

I met a local farmer there, Peter, who was very willing to chat. I told him how I was so impressed with the beauty of Mullet Peninsula, and he agreed. ***"The last place God made"***, he said with pride. When I got to Rosbarnagh Island the causeway was covered so I decided that I would come back later with Maureen and Brian.

(We returned to the island on the Monday afternoon. Strava recorded our complete circle of the island as only 2.5km but it was tough going with no real path to follow and lots of ditches, long grass, and fences to climb over.)

Meanwhile on this Saturday morning, running on my own, I kept to the country roads. I coasted around the village of Binghamstown which at one stage was the main centre of population on the peninsula. The village was founded by Major Bingham (not sure if he was related to the North Down Binghams). The major didn't take too kindly when a rival town, Belmullet, was built and so he erected a large gate across the roadway to stop anyone who took their animals to the Belmullet Fair. They had to pay a toll as they passed through his gate. It became known as *An Geata Mhor* (the big Gate)

So being the rebel that I am, I avoided Binghamstown and any possible toll charge! In any case my coastal route was much more interesting even if it did mean crossing a rough trail which I spotted as a dotted line on the Ordnance map. Soon I arrived, feeling very thirsty, on the outskirts of the town of Belmullet. I stopped at a small garage, looking for water and the man in overalls asked me *"what kind of water do you want"*. I said, *"Water to drink"*. He told me he only had deionised water, so I decided to give that a miss and wait until I was able to get drinking water in a shop nearby.

I continued north, following the Ballyglass Road and taking an even quieter coastal lane. It was mostly a downhill run all the way to Ballyglass Pier.

I then backtracked a little and took a turn, signposted *Radharc na Mara* (view of the sea) which took me on a trail to Ballyglass Lighthouse where Maureen and Brian soon arrived.

STAGE 52

Co. Mayo: Mullet Peninsula: Ballyglass to Tra Bheal Doire

Sunday 11 July 2021

39.5 km or 24.5 miles

In the morning at the B&B I enjoyed some lovely poached eggs, mushrooms, and tomatoes. (I think it is over 30 years since I ate any red meat, so for me in the morning, it's usually eggs of some kind). After breakfast, Maureen and Brian drove me back to Ballyglass Lighthouse to start today's tough run. The Mullet Peninsula is quite flat with one exception, the northern top part which I happen to be tackling today.

Back at Ballyglass Lighthouse again

After leaving the lighthouse I'm able to run south on the country road. I don't risk taking the turn for Poll an Chapaill (stream of the horses) and trying to cross Blind Harbour. Instead, I stay on the main road and take a right, signposted Tipp Pier. I follow the coast all the way around, running through boggy fields. It seems to take me ages, but I eventually reach Ceann Iorrais (Erris Head) where I had arranged to meet Maureen and Brian again.

At Erris Head, Maureen and I get talking to two girls, Helen and Ali who are doing their own walking and swimming challenge around the peninsula. Helen is commemorating her sister and brother (Tish and Niall Murphy) who tragically lost their lives in a drowning accident exactly twenty years ago. We also get to talk to Cathal and Noreen at the kiosk/coffee stand (Cliffside Treats). Noreen had her own personal tragedy when she lost her son, Daniel, in a fishing accident. We had seen a commemoration plaque for Daniel on Rinroe Beach a few weeks ago and coincidentally it was Stephen (landlord from Yellow Rose B&B where we stayed) who found Daniel's body after he was missing for days.

Brian & Maureen during loop walk at top of Mullet Peninsula

Maureen and Brian join me along a 5km official trail, and I appreciated walking (rather than running) for a few miles. After we reached the northern tip of the peninsula, I say goodbye and head south on the coastal headland. This was tough going but it did take me close to Eagle Island (Oilean Tuaidh).

A Goat's Song

I've just been reading Dermot Healy's book *'A Goat's Song'* and he refers to this particular area. It's the perfect novel to read if you are visiting the Mullet Peninsula. The main character in the book had a house in Aghadoon and he refers to Eagle Island and its flashing light from the lighthouse **'*three times flashes, count to eight and three times more*'**. At night from our B&B (10km away) we can see the flashing Lighthouse, but Brian and I counted to eighteen (not eight) each time before it flashes again!

I stayed by the coast and finally arrived at Dun na mBo (the cattle fort). In older times this was some kind of strategic fortress. There is a blowhole here where the water is pushed forty metres up from sea level and sometimes stones are scattered around. It's low tide now and so it means I can take a shortcut along a strand that eventually brings me onto the road towards Annagh Head.

Annagh Head (Ceann an Eanaigh)

I ran all the way down to the end of the peninsula at Annagh Head. Here on the west side of the Mullet Peninsula are the oldest rocks on mainland Ireland, 1,753 million years old. In the book *'A Goat's Song'*, people light a bonfire at Annagh Head to celebrate St. John's Night (23rd June). However, today I'm the only person here and feeling very young compared to the ancient rocks!

I leave Ceann an Eanaigh and backtrack along the road. Soon I notice sand dunes on my right, so I climb a fence and suddenly find myself on another pretty beach. I'm on the sandy west side of the Mullet Peninsula. I can see Carne Golf links often ranked as Ireland's favourite, by those curious enough to venture this far west.

It's not all easy along the strand but it is mostly beaches (or sand dunes) and I eventually arrive at Tra Bheal Doire. It's 6.00pm and it's been a long day!

STAGE 53

Co. Mayo: Mullet Peninsula: Tra Bheal Doire to Tra Deirbhile

Wednesday 14 July 2021

17.2 km or 10.7 miles

Today Maureen and Brian joined me for the first three kilometers, which was just a nice walk on the beach. Even when I left them, it was mostly a 16k run along the strand on the west side of the peninsula.

Interestingly we followed some of the route for the Erris parkrun but because of Covid restrictions the parkrun has not started back yet. At Blacksod Pier on Monday morning I happened to bump into the organiser of the Erris parkrun, Padraig Brogan, and I promised I would come back when it restarts. Padraig insisted that I come into his office later that day and presented me with a parkrun cup and an Erris parkrun keyring. In January 2023 I was shocked to hear the very sad news that Padraig had passed away. I was so privileged to have met such a lovely man. I still carry the Erris parkrun keyring with me, attached to my car and house keys. I will keep my promise to return some day and do the parkrun in Padraig's honour.

Sinead Diver

Speaking of running I realise I'm not too far away from where Sinead Diver grew up. Sinead is running in the Tokyo marathon in a few weeks. She only started running in

2010 at the age of 33 after she moved to Australia. Under normal circumstances she might have been home here in Corclough and might have even joined me, but I'll excuse her today as she's running at a much bigger event in Japan! And an update to this story: Sinead finished tenth in the Olympic Marathon in August 2021 in a time of 2 hours 31 mins. More recently in December 2022 she knocked another 10 minutes of that time in the Valencia Marathon with 2 hours 21 mins. That time would have won her every Olympic Marathon. Not bad for a wee girl from the Mullet peninsula.

Inish Gluaire Island & its legends

Across the sea, I can clearly see Inish Gluaire (The island of Purity) which has a connection to the *'The Children of Lir'*, an old Irish legend about four children who were turned into swans. Inish Gluaire is where, according to the story, the swans/children had to spend the final 300 years, as part of their punishment.

There is another even stranger and scarier legend that the medieval writer, Giraldus Cambrensis (1146-1223) tells about Inish Gluaire island. It says that human corpses don't decay on the island and *'if deposited in open air, they remain uncorrupted; relatives can recognise their parents, grandfathers, and all their ancestors'.* Not so sure if I want to believe this. It reminds me of the *'White Walkers'* in Game of Thrones which would give anyone the creeps!

Anyway, back to this century and July 2021. I say goodbye to Maureen and Brian and continue along the beach. Soon I come to a stretch of the coast that is quite rocky. The local farmer has done such a brilliant job with his barbed wire fencing, meaning I can't even run in the fields. I have no alternative but to climb over the rocks and boulders which seem to take me ages.

However, once I've tackled that rocky section, I have a beautiful sandy section ahead. The beach is about 3.5km long and I recognise it as I was here at this exact spot yesterday with Maureen and Brian.

On west side of Mullet Peninsula

Inishkea Islands

From the west coast of the Mullet peninsula there are lovely views across to the Inishkea islands. I've had a fascination with these two islands for about twenty years, even before I knew exactly where Inishkea was. My curiosity came from the fact that these twin islands seemed to buck the trend as regards the population decreasing after the famine. The potato blight never reached Inishkea. The islanders also had a great tradition and skill with fishing. Furthermore, in the early 20th century when other areas had high emigration, a Norwegian whaling station brought employment to Inishkea.

Brian gets a chance to drive the boat to Inishkea

Although Inishkea avoided the famine they were met with a terribly tragedy in 1927 when a massive storm claimed the lives of ten fisherman. After this disaster, the islanders realised that it was no longer safe to be fighting the hazardous Atlantic winds. Both of the Inishkea islands were then abandoned.

Maureen, Brian, and I were delighted to be able to visit Inishkea South on Tuesday. I resisted the temptation to run around the island although it would have been quite an easy challenge. For our trip we were blessed with a beautiful day and a lovely calm see crossing. The island (Inishkea South) was everything I wished for. We had four hours to explore it all and enjoy our picnic in this magical Atlantic isle! The ruins of the old houses still remain, and it was easy to imagine hundreds of villagers living here just a century ago.

Meanwhile back to today: On the western shore of the Mullet peninsula, I continue along the beautiful beach, then take a sandy trail that joins up with the country road and arrive at the townland of Glais.

After the great storm in 1927, most of the Inishkea islanders were relocated to this area. I also noticed a place nearby on the map called *'An Baile Nua'* (new town). It's the perfect downhill run to my finish line at the pier (An Port Mor) and then along the strand to Tra Deirbhile. Today was probably one of my nicest runs so far, mostly beach and perfect ***'sand for the feet of the runner'***. Across the sea I can clearly see the hills of Achill Island. Dark Slievemore is towering above and the huge cliffs of Croaghaun are leaning into the sea. It's going to be tough going when I get to Achill. However, that's a run for another day.

STAGE 54

❖

Co. Mayo: Mullet Peninsula: Tra Deirbhile to Clogher

Monday 12 July 2021

13.7 km or 8.5 miles

I began today's run at the B&B (Bru Chlann Lir) near Clogher and completed this section clockwise. I had two tough days of running so I was struggling to get moving at all today. Just as I did on Saturday, I headed down to Tra Mullach Rua. When I got to the beach, I ran south this time and then later I re-joined the main road.

As I was running down to Blacksod Pier I noticed a group of people gathered there. I thought that, maybe word had got around that I was running around the Mullet peninsula. Unfortunately, the small crowd were <u>not</u> there to greet me. They were waiting for a government minister, Jack Chambers, to arrive as there are plans to open up the Blacksod Lighthouse as a museum. I got talking to a freelance journalist, Tom Reilly (from Takemeschnap) who, having time to kill before the minister arrived, did a video interview with me. I told him my story and later I was able to share the video link on my Facebook page.

There is so much history here on the Mullet Peninsula and as I'm running around the coast of Ireland, I'm always conscious of those who have suffered in various battles or disasters. However, when something happens in more recent times it's more difficult to refer to it. On 14 March 2017, a rescue helicopter had completed the medical evacuation of an injured fisherman 250 kilometers west of Blacksod. On returning to the Mullet peninsula the aircraft crashed into a high island called Blackrock Island, about 17km west of the peninsula. Sadly, all four crew members on board, Dara Fitzpatrick, Mark Duffy, Paul Ormsby, and Ciarán Smith died. Captain Shivnen spoke at the service of Paul Ormsby whose body was never recovered and said the following.

'You are a rumble in the sky: you are a flickering star: you are hope in the darkness'

Plaque at Blacksod Pier with names of four lost at sea

The D Day Landings

It's amazing that Blacksod and the Mullet peninsula has a connection to the D Day Landings. In 1944 Maureen and Ted Sweeney, who worked at the local weather station in Blacksod Bay, were first to forecast a severe Atlantic storm, which led to a change of plan in one of the world's biggest military operations. Maureen Sweeney only died recently in December 2023 at the great age of 100 years. She liked to tell the story about what happened in June 1944 and how the D Day Landings were postponed for one day because of their knowledge of the local weather conditions.

> *'A lady with a distinct English accent requested me to 'please check. please repeat'. We checked and rechecked and the figures were the same both times. They would have gone ahead, and the invasion would have been a complete disaster. There they were, with thousands of aircraft which couldn't tolerate low clouds. They could arrange everything, but they couldn't pre-arrange the weather! We were delighted we put them on the right road.'*

Back in 2021 as the government minister arrives at Blacksod Pier, I decide it's time for me to leave and head towards the beach where I'm finishing today's short stage. Legend says Saint Deirbhile travelled here to this part of Mayo to escape a lover. Yes, you can't get much further away than this corner of the Mullet Peninsula! It's a charming south facing beach and I'm glad to soak my feet in the salty water until Maureen and Brian arrive.

Total coastal circle of Mullet Peninsula: 116.7km or 72.5miles

STAGE 55

Co. Mayo: Belmullet to Gaoth Saile

Saturday 14 Aug. 2021

41km or 25.5miles

'Isn't there the light of seven heavens in your heart alone and I abroad in the darkness, spearing salmons in the Owen, or the Carrowmore' John Millington Synge from 'Playboy of the Western World'

I think Maureen, Brian and I fell in love with the Mullet Peninsula in July. This time we are staying at Kemar House, just west of Belmullet town. Our host, another Maureen, is looking after us and leaves out some Weetabix, milk and fruit for my early start. As I step outside the door at 6.20am I'm just in time to witness the most beautiful sunrise which gives me a spring in my step as I run towards Belmullet town.

Belmullet Town (Beal an Mhuirthead)

In 1822 William Henry Carter inherited many acres of land in northwest Mayo and built this new town. It impressed, Alexander Nimmo, a famous engineer who built harbours and piers all over Ireland.

> "At Belmullet, the advance is quite surprising; the place only commenced four years ago; it now consists of about seventy respectable houses"

In the 1830s, another visitor described Belmullet as *'the youngest town in Ireland and like all young things it is comparatively fresh and fair'*.

However, seventy years later Belmullet seemed to have let itself go. The famous written, John Millington Synge, visited Belmullet in 1904, and reported:

'Belmullet in the evening is noisy and squalid, lonely and crowded at the same time and without appeal to the imagination'

Of course, in those seventy years Ireland suffered its biggest natural disaster with the Great Famine in the 1840's. At one stage at the height of the Famine, 3,000 people were recorded as being in the local workhouse.

After leaving Belmullet I stuck to the Shore Road and ran past the outdoor Tidal Pool. We've noticed on previous visits how popular this unique swimming area is with all the young people. I take a left turn onto Cois Fhairraige which brings me up onto Church Road and I leave the Mullet peninsula by this quieter coastal road. I'm heading for Claggan Island.

Sign pointing to Claggan Island and Srah Beach

Claggan was only declared an island in 1991. In January of that year there was a windstorm from the Atlantic that cut off the island from the mainland for days. Even the tombola (a long bar of sand) stretching to the island was covered by the incoming sea. Today, I have no obstacles as I run along the sandy ridge. On the island itself the old Coastguard Station has been renovated by the Howard family. They converted it into self-catering accommodation and glamping pods. I was delighted to meet father and son, both called Laurence Howard, who had a very warm welcome for me.

I had heard about a sculpture on the island that commemorated the unbaptised who were buried on the island. Both men took me to see it. These burial sites are called cillíns and in a field on Claggan Island there is a mound of earth where those that were *'declared unworthy'* were buried. A sculpture by the artist, Marian O'Donnell's consists of two curved stone walls facing each other but separated from each other by a narrow passageway.

Cillin Sculpture showing passage between two curved walls

I was privileged to be able to walk between the two stone walls which symbolises that you are embracing, protecting, and acknowledging those buried in the cillín. I came across a similar island in Donegal, called Oilean na Marbh (Island of dead) where hundreds of babies were buried. (See stage 28 in my Ulster Coastal Run book). Here in Claggan Island there is a poignant inscription by the poet Derek Mahon

> ***'They are begging us to see in their wordless way, to do something, to speak on their behalf, or at least not to close the door again'***

I could have chatted to the two Laurence's all day. They were so modest, yet so proud to show me around. Yes, Claggan Island is a special place, and it was such a lovely encounter with these two gentlemen.

Keeping the sea on my right, as always, I left the island and ran along the strand on the other side (Srah beach) of the tombola.

The road eventually brought me to Doolough (Dumha Locha) strand. This beach is famous for the annual horse racing (and greyhound racing) which takes place every year. In fact, this is the weekend that the event should have been taking place. Unfortunately, due to Covid, it is cancelled again. I was struggling at this stage and slightly envious of the horses and greyhounds with four (rather than two) long legs to gallop on the strand.

Along the beach I met a man called Mervyn who advised me to follow a track inland that would lead to a road. To my detriment I ignored his good advice and ended up running through a maze of sand dunes. My Strava record of today's run literally shows me running around in circles in those dunes!

Eventually (yes that one word 'eventually' that covers a lot of time and frustration!) I was able to spot in the distance a few houses. I climbed a fence, ran along a farmer's track, and made my way up to a country road. The rain is starting to fall just as I arrive in Gaoth Saile.

STAGE 56

Co. Mayo: Gaoth Saile to Bangor Erris

Sunday 15 August 2021

34km or 21.1 miles

Today was my earliest start to any of my coastal runs. I'm up at 5.00am, sneaking out of the room and trying not to wake Maureen and Brian. I had a light breakfast (Weetabix and fruit) at the B&B, drove the 18km from Belmullet to Gaoth Saile and started my run just as dawn was breaking at 5.50am. I had realised that the first 20km of my run today would take me on a complete loop around Dumha Thuama peninsula. I was in plenty of in time to return for my cooked breakfast (scrambled egg) at 9.00am. Evelyn at the B&B confirmed that I was the only person to ever have two breakfasts in Kemar Guesthouse!

Everyone is smiling this morning and talking about Mayo's great win in the All-Ireland semi-final last night which ended Dublin's seven-in-a-row attempt to keep the Sam Maguire cup. The Saw Doctors *'Green and Red of Mayo'* has been playing all day on Mid-West Radio and there's a lovely atmosphere all over Erris.

Brian at Mayo car just before their great win over Dublin

Gaoth Saile

It's very quiet here at 5.50am as I get out of my car. I get the impression that even at 5.50 in the afternoon things would not be much different in this remote village. The writer John Millington Synge has connections to this area. *'The Playboy of the Western World'* was inspired by a 'shebeen' in Gaoth Saile, which Synge described as 'very rough and untidy'. To further emphasise the wild-west image in the village there is a pub here called *'The High Chaparral'* (after the 1960's TV series) which caught me by surprise.

I'm tackling this Doohoma peninsula today and follow a sign for Radharc na Mara that brings me down to Doohoma beach. Over 5,000 years ago this whole area was covered by a great forest of oak, yew, and pine. It's just 7.00am now as I reach this secluded beach. Towering Slievemore on Achill is facing me across the bay, almost winking at me and saying, *'see you next month'*. I'm not sure if I'm looking forward to it.

Translated it says 'He who travels has stories to tell'

I passed a small monument dedicated to Seamus Mag Uidhir (Jim Paddy) who was from Doohoma and travelled all over Mayo on his bicycle in the 1930s.

Doohoma Cemetery

Like most of Connacht, this area suffered so much because of the Famine. For years there was no proper cemetery here, so burials took place on the sand dunes. Calls for a proper graveyard were rejected by civil authorities so in 1926 a cemetery was built by voluntary work. In 1967 over 100 volunteers built a road from Doohoma village to the graveyard.

I carry on running south to the very bottom corner of the peninsula and pause again at Doohoma Head (An Ceann Ramhar). There were so many potato pickers from this area who went to Scotland each summer that some boats picked them up here at Doohoma Head.

There's a warm August breeze following me all day as I loop around the peninsula, and I can't help thinking of the direct translation of Gaoth Saile which is *'salty wind'*. It is still only 8.10am when I arrive back at the High Chaparral after my 22km circle of the peninsula. I have plenty of time to get back to Belmullet for my second breakfast.

We check out of the B&B and Maureen drives me back to Gaoth Saile to complete today's stage. Now it's a more straightforward 12km run along the west bank of the Owenmore River (or the big river, 'An Abhainn Mor' as its sometimes called). You could argue that Bangor Erris isn't really by the coast and perhaps I could have crossed the river earlier. However, I don't think there was any other option.

My legs are tired now as I tackle this winding road. What is keeping me going is the fact I'm soon going to achieve another milestone on this coastal adventure. Now I can say that I've run all the way from Bangor, Co. Down to Bangor, Co. Mayo.

STAGE 57

Co. Mayo: Bangor Erris to Ballycroy

Saturday 28 August 2021

45.7 km or 28.4 miles

'Feel the peace of heaven falling, as the stars shine through the valley. Whilst I sit and dream alone, a thousand miles from Ballycroy' Paul Gregan

We are based in Bangor Erris for the weekend after driving down from Bangor, Co. Down. That Bangor-to-Bangor connection helped me get a short interview with Tommy Marren on the local station in Mayo (Midwest Radio). As radio stations go this is one of the best and has a great mixture of news, local interest, and lovely music. We always tune in as soon as we cross the Mayo border.

Bangor Erris

The original name for the townland was Doire Choineadaigh (The Wood of the Kennedys). However Major Bingham (from Binghamstown on the Mullet peninsula) established a proper town here and called it Bangor Erris. In 1752 Dr. Pococke visited on his famous 'tour of Ireland' and, like me, stuck rigidly to the coast. He came *'when Belmullet was two day's journey west of Westport'*. Two days; that's not bad going at all, considering how long it's taken me to cover this area.

Bangor Erris is on the river Owenmore and is the first bridge over the river from the coast. However, I did feel guilty about missing out on an area called Aughness North on the southern shore of the river. Therefore, on the Friday night I convinced Maureen to drive me to Srahnamanragh Bridge (about 8 miles south of Bangor Erris) to complete this section.

It was still an early start on the Saturday. Evelyn our lovely hostess at Hillcrest B&B kindly got up and made me tea and toast. Dawn was breaking but the fog was still lingering as I hit the A59 road. However, as the morning went on, it cleared completely, and it turned out to be a beautiful day. At Srahnamanragh, I take a right turn just before the bridge and cover an area called Carrigeenmore ('big seaweed' which isn't very encouraging).

After circling the wee peninsula, I arrived back at Srahnamanragh Bridge in need of a drink. Lucky for me (in a moment of wisdom) I had planted a bottle of water here the night before. After quenching my thirst, I continued on the main A59 for only a few hundred metres and took a right turn signposted Creggane and Doona Castle

Doona or Fahy Castle

This castle has great historical significance as one of the most important ships of the Spanish Armada came to ground here in September 1588. The boat was called the *'Santa Maria Rata Encoronada'* and had 419 on board including many noblemen from famous Spanish families. The captain and crew spent a week here at Doona Castle and then set fire to the ship, destroying any evidence that they had been in the area, fearing they would be captured. Earlier in that same century the famous Queen Granuaile had seized the castle from the McMahon's in revenge for the killing of her lover, Hugh de Lacy.

I was not impressed with this historical site. Yes, it was in ruins but there was a relatively new house built just beside the castle. Also, there were a lot of *'private property'* signs around and absolutely no access to the famous castle. Maureen, Brian, and I even returned later, and we could only get to the nearby cemetery and see the remains of the old church. How disappointing this must be for visitors. A big sign on the main A59 road gives directions to the castle but as you get closer there's no indication as to how you can reach the ancient building.

I carry on running along the country roads and came to a dead end at Fahy or Corrignacloghmore. I then rough it through a farm and along the coast. I connect to the country road again heading towards Ballycroy. A car stops in front of me, and a man called Frankie Cormack jumps out *'Are you the Bangor-to-Bangor man'*, he says. He had heard me on MidWest Radio and kindly made a donation.

Frank also informs me that I have only one kilometre to go to my finishing point at Ballycroy Visitor Centre, which is great to hear. At the centre I enjoyed a lovely lunch (delicious quiche) with Maureen and Brian.

I had passed a sign earlier for *'Inis Bigil'*, just before Ballycroy and after lunch I suggested to Maureen that we drive down to a nearby pier at Doran's Point. We mentioned to a man at the harbour that we were curious about getting across to Inis Bigil. He shouted out to a boat that was already leaving the shore *'these people want to go too'*. The two boatmen, Michael and Timmy Leneghan returned to the pier and kindly took us on a magical trip over to the island.

The Leneghan brothers, Inis Bigil

The brothers are among eighteen people who still live on Inis Bigil. The island itself is tucked into a secluded bay, with Achill on the west side and Annagh Island on the east side. It's surrounded by hills, valleys, and mountains. The two Leneghan brothers had heard me on Midwest Radio and refused to take any money for the trip. They also made a donation, as did a man called David who had shouted at the boat to return. Maureen, Brian, and I spent a delightful 90 minutes exploring the beautiful island.

It is possible to drive (or run) across to the island but only when there are Spring Tides (extreme low tides). This crossing can be made from the southeast side of the island and by going through Annagh Island on the east side. I couldn't resist coming back again to run to this island at low tide.

Stage 57: Revisited: Inis Bigil and Annagh Island: Friday 1 September 2023: 11.8 km or 7.3 miles

The route I took through Annagh Island to Inis Bigil (the horse shaped island)

'The legacy of 'An Tailliur Gorm' will live on but who will be left to share Inis Bigil's poetry and stories to our future generation' (from a video 'A dying Culture')

Yes, I went back! I had to return to this mystic island and attempt to run across via Annagh Island at low tide. I convinced Maureen and Brian to join me on a return trip to Co. Mayo. This weekend there is a super blue moon, which will not be seen again for another fourteen years. Super moons occur when the moon reaches its closest point to the earth. We also know that a full the moon affects the tides and instigates an extremely low tide.

However, the day didn't start well. We were staying in Ballina and woke up to a very foggy morning. This was <u>not</u> good news as I knew I would be covering rough terrain and running along open sands. I had to be able to see exactly where I was going. Still, I knew low tide wasn't until 1.30pm so there was time for the fog to clear. About 10.00am the sun was trying to make an appearance and for the next hour or two there was a Fog versus Sun battle. Thankfully the sun eventually came out on top.

We left Ballina and drove south towards Ballycroy. About a mile south of the village we took a right turn at a small crossroads. We then came to a junction with a sign pointing straight ahead for Bellacragher Boat Club. In my original Stage 57, I ran down to the sailing club but this time we headed west to the shore.

It has turned out to be a beautiful sunny day. It's still only 12.15pm so we are at least a good hour before low tide. The plan is for me to try to walk across the narrow channel to Annagh Island, run for about a mile through that island, along a trail if I can find it. Then over the open sand (another 2km) to reach Inis Bigil Island. Easier said than done and a warning - please be very careful, if you're attempting this!

The problem was getting across the channel to Annagh Island. Even at 1.00pm it still looked too risky. I was able to walk along a sand bank that took me closer to the island but then the water was still quite deep and there was also a strong current. Maureen, Brian, and I waited and waited - and eventually saw the tide slowly recede.

Pointing out Hill of Corraun to Brian as I wait to cross to Annagh Island

At 1.30 it looked like the tide was still going out. At 2.00pm, we figured it was at its lowest and I could just about wade across to Annagh Island with the water just above my knees. The problem would be getting back again if I ran all the way to Inis Bigil, 3.5k away. As I didn't want to risk coming back to this narrow channel again, I made the decision that I would run all the way through Annagh Island to Inis Bigil and hopefully get a boat back from the north side of Inis Bigil to the mainland at Doran's Point. So, I said goodbye to Maureen and Brian and arranged to meet them later.

Arriving on Annagh Island and I've found the trail

Having finally reached Annagh Island I felt a sense of excitement to be on this strange isle that hardly gets a mention anywhere. I knew from the OS map that there was a trail through the island. I found the path quickly enough and started running, passing a forest on my left, and later meeting some sheep who stopped to stare at me. I eventually arrived on the west shore of the island. It was another good mile across a wet and sandy beach before I finally arrived onto the SE corner of Inis Bigil.

It was rough going as I ploughed through a few fields on Inis Bigil. I finally reached a path that brought me to the Church and then to the harbour. However, there was nobody at all about at Inis Bigil pier, just two empty boats. Maybe if I had any navigational skills at all,

I could have borrowed one of the boats and made it across to the mainland. Meanwhile Maureen had reached the pier at Doran's Point across the bay on the mainland. She rang me to say that it was deserted there too at her harbour. I waited on my side but still nobody turned up.

Two empty boats at Inis Bigil Pier

Luckily for me I remembered the Lenaghan brothers bringing us across to Inis Bigil in July 2021. I was able to google on my mobile phone and get their number. Michael answered the phone immediately, and I told him my story. As he was already on the island, he promised he would be with me in twenty minutes. He was true to his word. Fifteen minutes later the two Lenaghan brothers came to the rescue and took me in their boat back to the mainland. It is such an amazing journey crossing from Inis Bigil, especially on a beautiful day like today.

Michael Lenaghan and his brother to the rescue

The sea was calm and as we sailed across in this secluded bay, we were surrounded on all sides by the Mayo hills and mountains. The Lenaghan brothers treated me like the most important person in the world. As I sat in their boat, I felt like a king. I marveled at the beauty around me. It reminded me of the song about 'Bonnie Prince Charlie' who escaped to Skye after the defeat of the Jacobite Rising in 1745. ***'Carry the lad that's born to be King. Over the sea to Skye'.***

STAGE 58

Co. Mayo: Ballycroy to Achill Sound

Sunday 29 August 2021

37.0 km or 23.0 miles

It was back to Ballycroy National Park again to start today's run. I left Maureen and Brian and followed the road towards Inis Bigil Pier but took a left turn this time sticking to the quiet country coastal road.

I followed the signs south through this Drumgollagh area towards Bellacragher Boat Club and what a magical place I found. There was absolutely nobody here at this secluded oasis on a lovely Sunday morning. Then I saw a sign for a *'Solar walk'* which guided me over a wee bridge and onto an island (it doesn't seem to have a name so I'm calling it Bellacragher Island).

I followed a trail through the island with Achill Sound facing me across the narrow bay. On my solar walk, I passed signs for Venus and Pluto, and I felt like I could have been anywhere in the universe.

It's almost a shame to leave this lonely but lovely spot. Reluctantly I return to the crossroads at the top of the hill, take a right and then join up with the main N59 road. As I got closer to Mulranny, the road got steeper as it wound its way around Claggan Mountain. Still, I had the perfect downhill run at the end to Mulranny Park Hotel to meet Maureen and Brian. We sat for a while outside the hotel and then the three of us walked for a while along the Greenway towards Achill.

Such a beautiful route whether you're cycling, running, or walking along this 13k trail. It's very flat, away from any roads and so quiet and peaceful with beautiful views across Bellacragher Bay. This stretch of the Greenway covers the north coast of the Currane Peninsula and finishes just before the bridge on Achill Island. (it's recently been extended further into Achill). After a mile or two, Maureen and Brian turned back but I continued running. I know an area along here is called Tonragee, which translates as *'backside to the wind'*. Thankfully there's not even a breeze today and it's not long before I arrive in Achill with Stage 58 completed.

We are sad to be leaving this beautiful Erris area where we've been, on and off, since June. Just outside Bangor, we stop at a monument called The Crying Stone. This commemorates families that would have parted at this particular spot. Families would bid farewell to children emigrating or perhaps a wife would be seeing off her husband going over to Scotland, potato picking.

At the Crying Stone in Bangor Erris

Laherdaun

And we're still reluctant to leave the Erris area! Driving back to Ballina we take a right turn at Crossmolina and after about 9km we arrive in Laherdaun. There is so much history and interest in this one small village. As you drive towards Laherdaun the first thing you'll notice is the towering Nephin which is the highest stand-alone mountain in Ireland. It's over 800 metres high.

Brian with his well-deserved certificate for climbing Nephin

Brian was first to the top and we enjoyed the perfect views looking down on Lough Conn and the lovely valleys and hills below. We're really in the middle (and on top) of Co. Mayo. Brian was both cautious and nervous, but we took our time, especially on the way down. I was so proud of him, and he deserved his officially signed certificate that he received from Barrett's shop in the village.

Laherdaun has a sad history as fourteen young emigrants from the parish boarded the Titanic in 1912 at Cobh/Queenstown in Co. Cork. Only three of these young women survived the ill-fated journey. In the local church, every year on April 15 at 2.20am, eleven sombre tones ring out for those who died and three thundering strikes for the three women who survived.

Remembering Laherdaun eleven lost on Titanic

In 1798 General Humbert's forces passed through Laherdaun on their way to Castlebar. Humbert's small army of men arrived here at midnight and were lucky to have the help of a local priest, Father Andrew Conroy. Fr. Conroy had spent time at a seminary in Nantes and so had a good knowledge of French and was able to provide them with food and give important directions to Castlebar. Humbert and his men, although outnumbered by three to one, won a famous battle in Castlebar. However, later Father Conroy was arrested, tried, and executed by the British.

So, we leave Laherdaun and the majestic Nephin Mountain. I remember years ago seeing a play called *'The Country Boy'* set in this area. The play itself is about emigration and how people cope with living away from home. In the play one of the characters is not handling his new situation in New York very well and describes his homesick feelings as he pines for his beloved Mayo. *"Country boys are looking for something that's no longer there. When you're down on your luck and not a dime in your pocket, you can get a great view of the sun shining on the face of Nephin from Times Square."*

STAGE 59

Co. Mayo: Achill Sound to Mulranny

Saturday 11 Sept 2021

29.7 km or 18.4 miles

'One ought to go too far, in order to know how far one can, go' Heinrich Boll

Yes, it's the All-Ireland Final today and for most people in Mayo it's going to be a long day until throw in at 5.00 pm. Even, as a Galway man, I'm nervous so it's good to get a long run in before the big match. We're staying this weekend at Ostan Achill (Achill Island Hotel). We didn't intend to come here this weekend, but the lure of Co. Mayo tempted us back with the opportunity to be here if the county breaks that 70-year gap of winning the Sam Maguire Cup.

I grab a quick early breakfast at the hotel and quickly join the quieter country road heading south towards the bottom of the Corraun peninsula. I pass by a wee hill and river, both called Beal Feirste. Yes, I'm in Belfast, Co. Mayo!

Belfast, Co. Mayo with Hill of Corraun covered in mist behind

Soon I see a much bigger hill, Cnoc an Chorrain which dominates the whole peninsula. I run all the way down to the pier and meet a young couple who I get chatting too. It's a beautiful morning and this looks like the perfect place for fishing in this secluded spot.

I circle the grassy corner of the peninsula but struggle a little as its high tide now and not much sand to run on. Back on the coast road I stop to talk to a local man who tells me that there are two films being made in this beautiful area. One of them is called, ***My Sailor My Love***', by the Finnish Director, Klaus Haro and the other is '***The Banshees of Inisherin***' by Irish Director, Martin McDonough.

As I run around the southern part of the peninsula, I pass yet another Spanish Armada reminder. This one commemorates the ship, ***El Gran Grin*** *'* which sank nearby, off Clare Island.

Today has been a straight-forward run around this peninsula and soon I see Mullranny in the distance. I head down towards the beach and spot Maureen and Brian walking down from the Mullranny Park Hotel. It's perfect timing as I complete Stage 59.

Later in the afternoon we enjoyed a lovely dinner back in the hotel in Achill. We were able to catch the whole atmosphere in the bar as the All-Ireland Final started. Sadly, it wasn't to be Mayo's day. So, the adventure and search for Sam Maguire continues!

STAGE 60

Co. Mayo: Achill Sound to Doogort (Achill)

Sunday 12 Sept 2021

34.6 km or 21.5 miles

It's a beautiful morning as I set off on my run, crossing over the Michael Davitt Bridge and onto the island of Achill. Yesterday the two ladies who served me breakfast wore their Mayo shirts and snoods. Today they're back wearing their work blouses. Yes, a sad day for the county of Mayo after yesterday's All-Ireland loss.

I run along the main road for about a mile before taking a right turn onto the Shore Road, marked *'Saula Walk'*. I've heard of the Mayo Greenway being extended onto Achill Island and there are 'bike signs' along here. It is perfect for cycling, walking, or running.

Later I take a turn which takes me down to Bulls Mouth Pier. For over twenty years there was talk of having a cable-car across to Inis Bigil island. It's a pity it didn't take off as it would have opened Inis Bigil to tourism and would have promoted this side of Achill Island.

At the harbour I see a trail to my left which I follow along the coast. Unfortunately for me it's high tide now and I struggle through some rocks but get through to Dooinver Strand (Tra Dhun Ibhir). I keep running along the rocky shore, cursing Mother Nature and her incoming tide! I then come to *Loch Dhun Ibhir*, and things get even worse. The tide is so far in that it joins up with the lake and there's no obvious way across. In hindsight I should have taken off my shoes and socks to the other side and probably would have made it across. Being sensible I decided to double back, head inland and follow the road around the lake.

However, I went too far inland, and I calculate that my round trip (around Loch Sruhill) cost me an extra 4km. I run down towards the sea again and I'm able to follow a perfect coastal trail that brings me all the way to Ridge Point (Gob an Iomaire) which is Achill's most northerly point.

Even when that path comes to an end, I can rough it for a short while through some fields before joining up with two lovely beaches at Gubnahardia and later, Golden Strand which is sometimes called, *'Bhearna na gCapall'* (strand of the horses). A study done on this strand recently revealed that, even though Golden Strand was battered by seventeen storms, it was 'largely insensitive' to their impact. This sand might be dragged away in winter by these blizzards, but it is held offshore and then returned in fair weather.

Yet another Cillin for the Unbaptised at Bhearna gCapall

Here I had to join the road again at Masterson's Bar and after a steep climb up the hill I arrived in Doogort and onto Pollawaddy strand where Maureen and Brian were there to meet me at my finish line.

STAGE 61

Co. Mayo: Achill: Doogort to Keel

Saturday 25 Sept 2021

36.7 km or 22.8 miles

'Achill called to me, as no other place had ever done' (the artist, Paul Henry)

I was delighted that my good friend, Sean Nickell joined me this weekend. I needed his ultra running experience over mountains and rough terrain. It was a long drive down to Achill Island on Friday night but at least we had the luxury of a beautiful guesthouse and delicious breakfasts supplied by Anne, our wonderful host in Joyce's Marian Villa at Keel Strand.

After a very hearty breakfast, Sean and I drove the short distance from Keel to Doogort (6km) to begin today's stage. There is a beautiful beach here, Pollawaddy Strand, at the foot of towering Slievemore. In 1831, evangelist Edward Nangle arrived in Doogart and build slated houses, a printing press, a hospital, a post office, and a corn mill. However, it does look as if the village has declined from those early glory years. Even the Strand Hotel, which has the perfect setting on the beach, looks as if it has seen better days.

Getting ready to circle Slievemore with Sean

Still the spectacular natural beauty of Doogart beach and Slievemore mountain (672 metres high) remains. Unfortunately, today the top half of the mountain is covered in mist and clouds. We started our climb near the hotel, following the coastal lane which ends abruptly at a pier. From then on, it was a matter of sticking to narrow sheep tracks as we circled Slievemore. We came around the west side of the mountain at Ooghnadirka and eventually we made our way downhill. Below in the valley, we could clearly see a row of abandoned houses which is Achill's *'Deserted Village'*.

Achill's Deserted Village

The tiny houses were probably only occupied in the summer when cattle would be grazed on the mountainside. This was called *'booleying'* and usually residents would return to their own house in Pollagh and Dooagh for the winter.

Keeping the sea on our right, heading towards Annagh Strand, Sean and I stayed further north of the deserted village, sticking to the coast. Soon we had to climb another hill, Cornaclea (269 metres) In the distance we can at last see Lough Nakeeroge and the charming Annagh Strand. There was no easy access down to the beach, so Sean and I had a tricky downhill walk through the heather. It was all worth it and we had our first break of the day on this beautiful spot in the wilderness. On google maps, this is now called

'Achill Island's Secret Beach'. (I should never have told my son Matthew, who works for Google, about this!) Annagh was also referred to as ***'The Back of Beyond'*** after a short story by T. Barry and that is a good description of this area.

Way in the distance, we see a couple of men herding sheep. They must have climbed over hills and through fields as there are absolutely no roads or lanes in this area. They might be modern day 'booley' farmers. We stick close to the coast now and stay north of Lough Nakeeroge, Tinny Lough and Bunafreva East. We've been walking most of the day up to now but suddenly Sean breaks into a quick trot along these narrow sheep trails. He falls over unceremoniously and I laugh. (About an hour later, Sean has the last laugh as I try running through some boggy long grass and fall flat on my face)

Eventually we reach the NW corner of Achill which is called Saddle Head. The sun has come out now and we can see the long stretch of the Mullet peninsula. I'm thinking of the book, the Goat's Song by Dermot Healy. One of the main characters in the book spots the beautiful Mullet peninsula from Achill and asks, ***'What's thon island I can see from here'***.

At Saddle Head - looking across at Cliffs of Croughane

Although Saddle Head is now basked in sunshine, it's another story as we look south. We can see the towering cliffs of Croaghane, but the tops are covered in thick fog and our plan to stick to the coast today looks not only tricky, but treacherous. We try to access the cliffs a little further inland, and we climb higher and higher, but the fog gets thicker and thicker. Eventually we do make it all the way up to a small lake, Bunnafreva Lough West (318 metres high). The Irish naturalist Robert Lloyd Praeger said that this lake was, *'so lonely and sterile and primeval that one might expect to see the piast or another Irish water-monster rising from the inky depths'.* It is indeed an eerie place here by the mountainous lough, surrounded by intimidating cliffs. Today, shrouded in thick fog, it looks even more 'lonely and sterile'. As we ponder here at Lough Bunnafreva West, the temperature is dropping, and our hands are getting cold. We decide that it would be foolish to climb up any further and so we make a sensible decision to turn around and descend about 250 metres.

Trying to avoid and get around the fog, we ended up going all the way back to Lough Nakeeroge and climbing over the hills. This route brought us eventually through a long boggy field and to a row of holiday homes called Corrymore Village about 3km east of Keem strand. With so few people around, I couldn't help thinking that this was like a modern version of a *'deserted village'.*

It was about 5.30pm now and we had a steep run down to Keem Strand. All I was thinking about was taking my shoes off, washing my filthy feet in the salty water, and changing into a spare pair of socks. Yes, it felt good having a fresh pair of feet for the last part of today's adventure. We made our way (walking) back up the steep hill and then had a perfect downhill run all the way to the village of Dooagh.

The artist Paul Henry lived nearby and fell in love with Achill. He only came for a holiday but dramatically threw his return ticket into the sea here in Dooagh. Also in this area, the writer, Graham Greene, not only fell in love with Achill, but also fell for Catherine Walston. The book and film *'The End of the Affair'* covers their passionate relationship.

Dooagh Strand became famous in 2017 because the beach reappeared after being 'missing' for thirty years. Sean and I did try to run along the shore, but it looks like the beach has disappeared again! Daylight is also fading now as we eventually reach our destination at Joyces Guesthouse in Keel.

Stage 61- Revisited: Achill: Croaghaun Cliffs: Sat,10 June 2023: 16.6km or 10.3miles

'Achill, wind-swept and bare, with great gaunt brown mountains rising here and there, and a wild coast hammered by the Atlantic waves on all sides.'
Robert Lloyd Praeger

Back in September 2021 when Sean Nickell and I were in Achill we tried unsuccessfully to climb these cliffs, the highest in all of Ireland. The cliffs were steep, and the fog was getting thicker and the air colder. The historian, Praeger was correct in calling this a **'lonely and sterile place'**. For Sean and me, the low cloud added to the scary atmosphere. We didn't delay and it would have been treacherous to climb any higher.

There was an even earlier account of this mountain lough by Edward Newman in 1838. **'Near the margin of the cliff a beautiful little fresh-water lake, surrounded by an amphitheater of hills. Its surface was 1,000 feet above the sea. I doubt whether any Englishman but myself has ever seen this lone and beautiful sheet of water'**

Still, I knew had to go back! Not only to climb those famous cliffs but to try to reach that lake again, Bunnafreva Lough West (or Loch Reithi Dubha). So, twenty-one months later I returned to Achill with my son, Matthew.

The mist and fog do seem to be clearing as Matthew and I start our hike from the beach at Keem Strand. We walk up the main road for about 2km and then take a left turn and ascend another 1.5km until we reach Lough Acorrymore. It's only when we get up as far as the 500-metre point that the fog slowly engulfs us. Now we must try to locate the elusive **'Bunnafreva Lough West'** that Sean and I had reached in 2021. It was not easy to find it. Lucky for me I had my son Matthew with me. He was able to pick up a satellite connection and eventually, despite the heavy fog, we found the **'beautiful little fresh-water lake'**, described by the Englishman, Newman in 1838. We were able to look down from our height of 510 metres to the lake below which was 318 metres. The lough was still barely visible in the fog but that round shape makes it easily recognisable. I was now satisfied that I reconnected to the original run I did with Sean Nickell in September 2021.

Today, for Matthew and me, the coast then became our compass as we headed south. Normally, I would say, 'stick to the coast' but in this case, it's safer not to get too close. After a while we had to climb even higher as we maneuvered our way through rocks until we finally reached the highest point on the island at 688 metres (2,257 feet). The good news was that the fog was lifting as we descended, and the sun was starting to break through.

Wee Matthew with giant cliffs behind him

I had forgotten how hilly Achill is. We cross a narrow river at Ooghnagertleen and head west towards Achill Head in the SW corner of the island. I was determined to reach the tip of Achill Head (it looked easy on the map). However, to be here and witness the narrow, broken ridgeways that lead to the head was another story. It looked treacherous to walk across the ridge. We did attempt one section but quickly realised that it would be foolish to go any further.

The route (to Achill Head) not taken!

Up to now I've had a very good relationship with sheep on my coastal runs. Cows I don't like, but sheep usually jog out of the way. However, near Achill Head, Matthew and I met an aggressive ram! The ram stared at us and prepared a marching stance, like a bull. He had the horns too. Unfortunately for Mathew and me we were very near the edge of the cliff when the ram confronted us. I also took off my rucksack, preparing to use it as a weapon if necessary. After a while, the ram calmed down, slowly moved out of our way and, with relief, we were able to continue.

We can see Keem Strand in the distance and the remains of Captain Boycott's house on the hill above. I knew the story about the man with the notorious name but didn't realise he lived here or that he was only a land agent rather than a landlord. Some land agents were stricter than others in making sure monies were collected and Boycott fell into this category. An opportunity for him came in 1872, when John Crichton, who owned 2,184 acres in Mayo, offered him the agency of lands near the Neale, Co. Mayo, and a lease on a farm of 629 acres with a good house, stables, a ruined castle, two islands, a boathouse and sporting rights. Sounded like a job-offer he couldn't refuse.

Boycott relished the task and became a very strict land agent. Despite poor harvests he insisted that tenants paid their full rents. As it happened the Land League protests were just starting at that time, led by Michael Davitt. These were peaceful demonstrations which eventually led to a campaign where local shops refused to serve Captain Boycott and his estate. Soon the story became nationwide, and his name came into the English language. Boycott never recovered from the humiliation.

Matthew and I still had to reach Moyteoge Head. There are light drops of rain, but we don't mind as we know our finish line is close. When we finally reach Keem Strand, we dip our feet in the sea. After today's adventure, Matthew and I drove to Keel and stopped off for a lovely meal at *'The Amethyst Bar'*. Afterwards we even stocked up on Achill's secret spring water. No drink ever tasted as good!

STAGE 62

❖

Co. Mayo: Achill: Keel to Achill Sound

Sunday 26 Sept 2021:

31.1 km or 19.3 miles

'A soft day, thank God. A wind from the south with a honeyed mouth; a scent of drenching leaves' Winfred M Letts

Sean and I woke early this morning to the sound of strong winds and heavy rain. We took our time over breakfast as we watched it pour outside. Joyces Guesthouse is on a lane leading to the beach so we're quickly running along Keel Strand.

As we headed south towards the end of the long beach, Sean spotted a cliff path up on the hill. Once we reached that high trail, we had the option of climbing even higher as far as Minaun Heights (466 metres high). We could clearly see the transmission masts and we knew that, if we reached Minaun, we would be able to follow a country road for the rest of the day. However, as it was clearing up, we decided to rough it further south and follow the cliff path, strictly by the coast of course. It turned out to be a great decision. The landscape along here was spectacular.

I notice on the Ordnance Survey map that this area is called *'An tAlt Dearg'* (the red place). Speaking to Anne at the B&B she showed us amazing pictures of these cliffs in a fiery red colour. It's really a deceptive appearance from the evening sun shining on the Minaun Cliffs which creates a vivid red colour. This is like the Bloody Foreland in west Donegal where the rock face shows a reddish illusion brought on by the evening sun.

Everything is turning in our favour now. The rain has stopped and the terrain with its short grass is perfect for running on. We make it all the way down to the bottom of Dooega Head (Ceann Dumha Eige)

Along here we pass two small memorials. One is marked just 'Raymond', but I think it's for Raymond McKenna who went missing in this area exactly ten years ago. The other memorial we pass is in memory of crew members of the *Lios Garra* fishing boat which sunk near here in 1979.

Memorial at Dooega of Thomas Patten

Shortly we arrive in the seaside village of Dooega (Dumha Eige). We pass a monument dedicated to Thomas Patten who was the first Irishman to lose his life in the Spanish Civil War. He was one of many young men who fought with the Fifteen Brigade against the fascist Franco regime. Christy Moore referred to him in his song, *'Viva La Quince Brigade'.*

We're now able to follow the quiet road that loops around the southern part of Achill. After two days of mountain and hill climbing, my legs are suffering but at least it's relatively flat from now on, well except for one last steep hill at *'Port na hAille'* (beautiful bay). With the sun now making an appearance it is indeed a beautiful view. We spot Clare Island sitting majestically in the middle of the bay.

There is no fog at all now and Sean is cursing the fact that today (unlike yesterday) we could have got to the top of Slievemore and crossed over the Croaghane Cliffs. Suddenly, we come to a sign saying that the road is closed and blocked. I say to Sean, ***'I'm going through anyway. Nobody is going to stop this Coastal Run'***. It seems that they are making a film along here called ***'The Banshees of Inisherin'***. This is the movie starring Brendan Gleeson and Colin Farrell. We don't see any actual filming, but we pass a thatched pub, JJ Devine which seems to be part of the film set (We hear later that this pub was built especially for the movie).

Shortly we arrive at the most southerly point of Achill Island at Cloughmore (An Chloic Mhor). Just off the southern point is Achillbeg which is now uninhabited since the 1960's. There had been one hundred inhabitants on this island in 1900 but even in the 1950's all eight pupils in the school were siblings.

What a beautiful day here at Cloughmore (SE Corner of Achill Island)

Heading north we can now see Achill Bridge in the distance. We pass Kildavnet Tower which is another one of Grainne O'Malley's castles. We run all the way to our finish line at Ostan Acail in Achill Sound and congratulate each other on our achievement. It's been a tough weekend. I've known for a while that this big island was going to be a huge test and it did push me to the limit. I was so glad to have the support of Sean on these wild and hilly shores of Achill.

STAGE 63

Co. Mayo: Mulranny to Newport

Tuesday 15 February 2022

28.6 km or 17.8 miles

'I am Raftery the poet full of hope and love with eyes that have no light, with silence unmoved. Going west on my journey by the light of my heart.' Anthony Raftery (the blind poet 1784-1835)

Maybe it wasn't such a good idea to restart my coastal run in February. Yes, I know it is officially the start of the Irish Spring but there were three named storms this week, Dudley, Eunice, and Franklin. Luckily for me, Storm Dudley did not live up to expectations and I was able to squeeze in my three runs before Eunice and Franklin arrived. It took me 58km to cover the coastal route from Mullranny to Westport which is only 29km by road.

Like the blind poet Raftery I am *'going west on my journey by the light of my heart'*. However, there were times over the last few weeks when I wondered if I would be running at all this month as I've picked up an injury.

The problem was self-inflicted and ended my long spell of injury-free running. One Sunday morning in late November I turned on my foot and sprained my ankle. It even happened on one of my favourite trails to Helens Tower (with my favourite Sunday Morning Running Group) and not far from where I live in Bangor, Co. Down. I really should blame the late Lord Dufferin for my accident. He instigated this 8 km long trail through the forest that links Helens Tower (built in 1848) to Helens Bay Railway Station. Dufferin even convinced one of his poet friends, Alfred Tennyson, to write a poem about Helen's Tower. Tennyson's dedication to the tower began ***'Here I stand, dominant over sea and land'***. Anyway, on the morning of my accident in the forest, I struggled home from Helen's Tower, feeling sorry for myself and making up my own verse. ***'Here I stood, hobbling through the lonely wood'***. My ankle grew bigger and bigger and later I had to reluctantly accept the fact that I needed a few weeks of complete rest.

So, today I'm not sure how far I can run and I'm being more cautious than usual after my long layoff. Furthermore Maureen, Brian and I have all recently contacted Covid and so we had to postpone this trip for a few days.

For practical reasons I've decided to do today's run clockwise with the sea on my left for a change. I'm starting my run at the end of a long peninsula/island (just west of Newport) that stretches out into Clew Bay at Rossmore Point.

I can see the island of Inishdaweel right in front of me. In the distance and in all directions lots of other islands are peeping out over the sea. The best view of the Clew Bay drumlins is from Croagh Patrick. Even if you only climb half-way up the mountain, you can see the beautiful sight of the islands spread out over the bay. I counted only about 60 or 70 from the Ordnance survey maps, not 365 as is commonly quoted. These drumlins are really the result of sea levels falling after the last ice age around 10,000 years ago. I remember seeing the same type of ***'drowned drumlins'*** in Strangford Lough when I completed the early stages of my coastal run.

Leaving Rosmore peninsula it takes me 3km to come back to the main road. I decide to run north with Lough Furnace on my left. I knew this route was not really by the coast, but I thought it would be more interesting to do a circular loop around the lake. After all, Newport is often called ***'Newport Furnace'***. The lough itself is unique because it consists of a lower layer of salt water and an upper layer of lighter fresh water. The highest point that can be seen in this area is Corranabinna which towers 714 metres, just 50 metres shorter than Croagh Patrick, but this mountain isn't even named on the Ordnance Survey map.

My diversion around Lough Furnace means that I don't pass Burrishoole Abbey, but I do come back later with Maureen and Brian to visit the impressive site and the old building. The Dominican Friars founded the Abbey in 1470 but they almost got excommunicated from the church because they didn't get permission from the Pope for its construction.

After running around Furnace Lough, I thought it was best to head inland towards the Mayo Greenway. Despite the miserable rain, I did feel better running along the old railway line. At least I have a traffic free run for the last 12k, and the Greenway takes me all the way to the Mullranny Park Hotel. Interestingly, the hotel is still owed by the Brown family who are direct descendants of the 16th century pirate Queen, Grace O'Malley. I just make it back to Mullranny before it gets dark, soaked to the skin at this stage. A hot shower later brought me back to life! In the morning from our Airbnb, we were able to admire Mullranny beach and look across to Croagh Patrick on the other side of Clew Bay.

STAGE 64

Co. Mayo: Newport to Rosmoney Pier

Wednesday 16 Feb 2022

15.5 km or 9.6 miles

'The day dawns with scent of must and rain, of opened soil, dark trees' Mirror in February by Thomas Kinsella,

Before I start my run, we spot a miniature 'lighthouse' at the end of the pier and a plaque with a poem called ***Echoes at Rosmoney*** by Ger Reidy. I read later that Ger wrote this in honour of his friend, Tommy Gibbons who tragically lost his life here at Rosmoney.

'You knew the whine of the wind at the point. The roar of the swell before a storm. These words now echo from island to island'

I leave Rosmoney Pier and follow the bike marker signs back towards Newport. Despite the forecast of heavy rain, it's very pleasant and the sun even makes the odd appearance. Around the corner I spot Croagh Patrick in the distance. I can see the famous cone-shaped mountain and I'm thinking of the lines from the Saw Doctors song ***from its rolling coastal waters, I can see Croagh Patrick's peak'***

I pass another one of Grace O'Malley (or Grainuaile) castles. Grainne was known as the pirate queen, and I often imagine her to be similar to the beautiful Daenerys Targaryen (the mother of dragons) in Game of Thrones

The cycle markers bring me past Kilmeena GAA Club (All Ireland Junior Club Champions in 2021) and all the way back to the main A59 road. Its only 5km to Newport and I'm able to follow the Greenway to today's finish point.

I make sure to cross over the majestic old railway bridge in Newport. The magnificent seven arch bridge was built in 1896 but by 1937 the trains stopped running as it was no longer economically viable to operate the railway.

Newport Furnace-Pratt or Ballyveaghan

Previously the town was called Newport Pratt after Captain Pratt introduced linen manufacturing in 1719. The linen weavers were part of a Quaker settlement in the area. Before that, Newport was originally called Ballyveaghan.

In 1976 Grace Kelly, the famous actress and princess, purchased her old family ancestral home in Drimurla, just outside Newport. She had planned to return to renovate it and perhaps live in it, but she had a fatal car accident in 1982. A wreath of wildflowers from Drimurla were sent by local people to Monaco for the funeral of the princess.

STAGE 65

Co. Mayo: Rosmoney/Inishcottle to Westport

Wednesday 17 Feb 2022

14.5 km or 9.0 miles

A lot of walking today, rather than running, with Maureen and Brian joining me. We got a little lost on the narrow country lanes and somehow ended up instead at the islands of Inishnakillew and Inishcottle. This turned out to be a blessing in disguise. When we reached Inishnakillew island we climbed up a narrow hill and had a magical experience right in the middle of Clew Bay. From the top of this hill, we had circular views of beautiful drumlins all around the bay.

View of drumlins over Clew Bay - from top of hill on Inishnakillew Island

Maybe we were lucky today with the calm before the storm because all these wee drumlins just sat there in front of us. We knew we were privileged to have a beautiful sight on such a perfect day.

<u>Inishturk Beg</u>: As you're walking up to the top of the hill on Inishnakillew island you'll spot Inishturk Beg on the right. A famous Irish-Egyptian businessman called Nadim Sadek bought the island for £1million in 2003. He snapped it up before other interested parties, like Ronan Keating, Bono and Bill Gates outbid him. Mr. Sadek spent a few more million on the islands properties but sold the island in 2013 for 4 million euro.

Maureen and Brian returned to the car, but I decided to run down the very steep hill and visit the connected island of Inishcottle. There was a small pier here, but the slipway just seemed to lead to a private house. As we were in an *'island hopping'* mood, the next challenge was to try to find Collan More (formerly Holly Island). After a while we took a right turn and drove down a narrow and very bumpy boreen, with lots of potholes. We got talking to a local man here who didn't think we could get across and back to the island as the tide was now turning. We took his advice.

Just west of Collan More is the wreck of a steamship, Charles Stewart Parnell. I'm not sure if I believe the story about the lobster that's still trapped in its boiler on the boat. Apparently, it grew too big to escape! All these islands surrounding Collan More make it a beautiful protected and secluded spot. It was up for sale at £500k, which seems a bargain compared to the much smaller Inishturk Beg (see earlier) which was going for 4 million euro.

I follow the country road east towards Westport. At least I have the wind behind me now and the rain is easing off too. Near here at Pigeon Point in 1894, a vessel carrying Achill Island *'tattie hokers'* - migrant harvesters bound for Scotland - overturned when all the young passengers rushed to one side of their boat to see a Glasgow-bound steamer. The boat capsized and thirty-two people were drowned.

I pass the golf course just outside Westport and eventually make my way through the centre of the town. Climbing the hill towards the coastal road I soon arrive at the Westport Woods Hotel. I'll start my next coastal run from here on St. Patrick's Day and the plan is to reach the top of Croagh Patrick on 17 March. Let us hope all the snow that we saw on the holy mountain has melted away by then.

STAGE 66

Co. Mayo: Westport to Louisburg (via Croagh Patrick)

Thursday 17 March 2022

38.4 km or 23.8 miles

'Walk with me westward along St. Patrick's Trail, along the pathway of the pagan, the passage of the pilgrim' John Corless

I'm delighted to have a few other runners join me over these two days. Donald Smith has travelled down with me all the way from Bangor. Helen Byers and Neill Weir are also going to meet us for the Croagh Patrick climb. Helen is of course one of the original coastal runners and has brought along her two children, Holly, and James (who have inherited their mother's determination). Finally, I got a lovely surprise on St. Patrick's morning when another runner turned up at the hotel. More about him later!

It's not a bad St. Patrick's Day and the forecast is promising for today's run and our climb up Croagh Patrick. Donald and I stayed at the Westport Woods Hotel last night and this is where we begin today's adventure. I needed to pop out to my car in the morning and I spotted someone outside that looked like Sean Nickell (original coastal runner). ***"Morning Gerry"***, he says. He sounded like Sean Nickell too! I'm dumbfounded and wondering if I'm still asleep and dreaming. Yes, it's definitely Sean and late last night he made the five-hour journey to get here. He slept overnight in his van (nick-named Bob after he converted it to a campervan) and now he's ready to join Donald and me.

From the hotel, Donald, Sean, and I follow the coast road all along Westport Quay and after about 4k we join the main road, R335.

We arrive at the foot of Croagh Patrick, which was originally called Cruchain Aighle (conical mountain). Yes, its unique shape makes the peak stand out for miles around. It is believed that in Year 441 St. Patrick fasted here on the mountain for 40 days.

Helen, Neill, Holly, and James are there to meet us at *'base camp'* and now we have a magnificent team of seven to begin our mountain of adventure.

The Magnificent Seven begin our climb of Croagh Patrick

Traditionally not many people climb the mountain in March. The historical annals for the year 1113 recount a St Patrick Day Pilgrimage where lightning struck and 'a ball of fire' killed 30 people who were fasting on the peak. Instead, the last Sunday in July has become *'Reek Sunday'* when thousands come here, usually in better weather. Yes, maybe it's not such a good idea to take on this task today as we later found out!

Even before we started our climb, we could see a lot of clouds at the top. I have to admit that I didn't have the appropriate clothing for this climb; a fact that was pointed out to me later by one of the bearded members of our own team. We struggled upwards through the rain, wind, and then foggy mist at the top. Donald tells us that the temperature drops by one degree for every 150 metres climb so for 764 metres that's a five degree drop. My three layers were soaked through. Sean told me later that I was in the first stage of hypothermia and I 'turned a funny colour'. Sean literally peeled my wet clothes off my body as my hands were too cold to even attempt it myself. Meanwhile Neill and Helen somehow had warmer clothes available to give me.

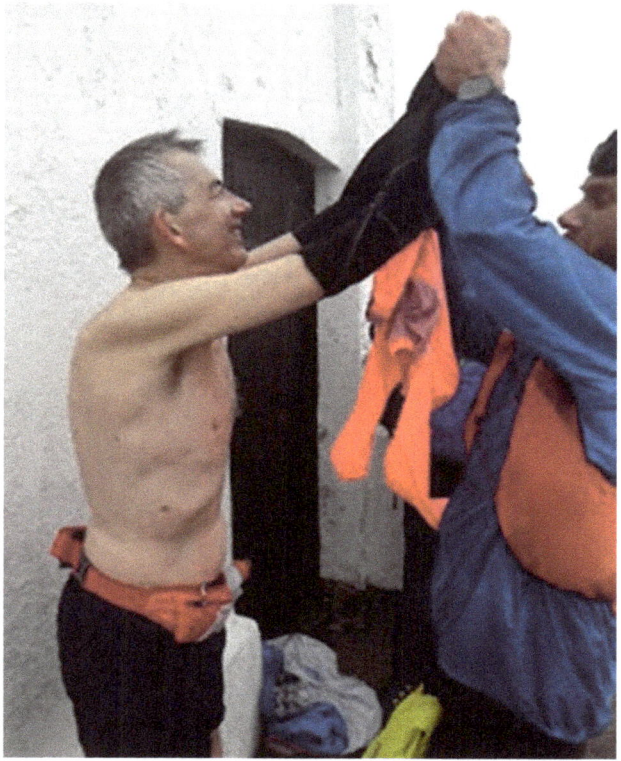

Sean Nickell undressing me at the top of Croagh Patrick

The church at the top was built by local men in 1905 using stone and cement brought up the mountain by donkeys. It would have been nice if the chapel was open today with central heated radiators and a big Aga cooker inside. Instead, we all huddled outside and used the wall of the church as protection from the elements.

There are no complaints at all from Helen's children, Holly (13) and James (11) who must be feeling the cold too. Despite the miserable weather they are both bouncing along and taking it all in their stride. I was delighted for their sake that the weather did pick up later as I knew they were going to tackle Mayo's beautiful greenway.

Back on Croagh Patrick, we didn't delay at the peak and quickly made our way downhill. Lucky for us, at the foot of the mountain, we found a pub, *'Campbells at the Reek'*, with a roaring fire inside.

So, the three elders leave the pub and run along the R335 and then take a right to Bertra Strand. We run all the way to the end of the long peninsula.

Dornish (John Lennon's Island)

Further north to our left we can see a long island, Dornish (this island can be easily seen from Croagh Patrick too). In 1967, John Lennon saw a newspaper advert *'island for sale'* and bought Dornish from Westport Harbour Board for £1,550. As his career progressed, Lennon postponed his moving to the small island and lend it to Sid Rawle, known as 'King of the Hippies'. In 1980 after John's death, Yoko sold the island for £30,000 and donated proceeds to an Irish Orphanage.

After coming back to Bertra beach, the three of us decide to stay on the shore along Thornhill Strand. At Lecanvey Pier, we run up the harbour road and join the main R335 again for about 4km and then take a lane (L18282) onto Fallduff Strand which brings us to Old Head Pier.

Sean, Donald, and I run up to the very top of Old Head itself but eventually the rough path gets narrower and precarious as we make our way along a steep cliff. We decide to come inland and clamber over a few fences and eventually find a country road that takes us all the way into Louisburgh.

Louisburgh

The First Marquess of Sligo named the town Louisburgh in memory of his uncle, Captain Henry Browne, who fought on the British side against the French in the battle of Louisburg, Nova Scotia in 1758. The Mayo town was originally called Kilgeever. I think I prefer this name which is now a townland outside Louisburgh. There used to be a *pilgrimage station'* at Kilgeever as it was on the route from Croagh Patrick to Caher Island, which makes sense. (See tomorrow's stage where I write more about Caher Island and its connection to St. Patrick)

At Louisburgh, we're so glad that Neill is there to drive us back to Westport. Later, all seven of us arrange to meet in the Towers Restaurant at the Harbour in Westport. I know I'm so privileged to have such great company and we discuss our various exploits of the day and plans for tomorrow. A delicious meal followed by Irish coffees finish off the day and night perfectly.

STAGE 67

Co. Mayo: Louisburgh to Louisburgh (out by coast and back by country road)

Friday 18 March 2022

43 km or 26.7 miles

"Will you meet me on Clare Island, Summer stars are in the sky. Get the ferry out from Roonah and wave all our cares goodbye" The Saw Doctors

You might wonder why today's run is a Louisburgh loop and why I haven't got any further along the coast. Let me explain. My original plan today was to try to get as far as Leenane, Co. Galway. I worried about the last part of this section along the north shore of Killary Harbour as you pass Connacht's highest mountain, Mweelrea. There is absolutely no road or trail along this section of the coastline, south of Uggool.

I struggled to find much detail about this area, but I knew one man who had walked here last year so I spoke to him. His name is Kieran O'Hora and in July 2021, in memory of his son, he walked the whole coastline of Mayo. I asked Kieran about this section, and he said of the entire walk around the coast of Mayo that this was the most daunting. He made a scary comment too about Killary Harbour *'the water is as deep as the mountain is high'*

I decided then that we would not follow the coastal route around Mweelrea but instead, head back along the country road and *'go around'* the mountain on the east side. Looking at the map I then realised that it made sense to run the whole way back to Louisburgh where we started from and where we could leave the car. Furthermore, it means that on my next stage, I'll now be able to follow the exact route from Louisburgh to Delphi that some malnourished families took during the Famine in 1849. This is also known as the *'Doolough Tragedy'*, and I'll detail it in my next stage.

Today we leave Louisburgh, cross the Bunowen River and follow this country road through Ashkillaun and down to Roonah Pier. There is boat just heading out to Clare Island and we're tempted to jump on it! Clare Island is by far the biggest island in Clew Bay and acts like a protector or guard of the bay by where it's situated. It's probably why the famous Pirate Queen, Grainne O'Malley (or Grainneuaile) made it her home. Literally, nothing coming into Mayo could get past her!

Ferry heading out from Roonah to Clare Island

Donald and I decide to try to stay on the coast at Roonah. We knew from the map that it was going to be rough going until we reached Carrowniskey Strand. We can clearly see the island of Caher and behind it is Mayo's Inishturk.

Caher is correctly called *'Cathair na Naomh'* (City of the Saints) and the island supported a small community of monks back in the seventh and eighth centuries. St. Patrick is said to have visited the island after he had been to nearby Croagh Patrick, and it is alleged that the famous saint is buried here on Caher Island. (The people at Downpatrick Cathedral might argue about that one!) For years, passing sailors were said to dip their sails on passing the island. They had profound respect for Patrick and referred to him as *'Phadraig miorbhuilteach'* (St Patrick the wonderworker).

Near Burlough Strand - Donald says we look like a Boyband in this picture

Finally, we arrive on a long beach called White Strand. We meet a couple here out walking. They are the Fitzgeralds from Athenry in Co. Galway. We tell them our story and they kindly made a very generous donation to our cause.

We carry on running along the long strand with a strong south wind in our faces. Soon we spot a man fishing on the beach, and we can see that there is something at the end of his line.

We stop to see what he's caught (just a wee flat turbot which he throws back into the sea). This is Peter Walsh the fisherman and Donald is pleased to meet a fellow Scotsman. Peter tells us about a nearby townland called 'Doirín na nAlbanach', *'the little thicket of the Scotsmen'*. Scottish shepherds were brought over in the 1860's by a lady called Matilda Houston.

We can see the lovely Silver Strand in the distance. (It's called Trawleckachoolia and Carrickwee on the OS map). The writer, Thackeray was equally impressed when he wrote to his mother after visiting this area, *'the most beautiful thing I have seen anywhere in Europe'*

Once we reach the beach, Donald and I sit and enjoy the moment. After a while we investigate if we could go further south along the coast towards the *'Lost valley of Uggool'* but there's a sign here that says, *'Preserved Area - No entry'*. I wasn't surprised when I saw this notice as I'd read that the landowner, Gerard Bourke doesn't allow access to his land. Anyway, I'm hoping to come back with Maureen and Brian to do the official tour of the 'Lost Valley'.

So, Donald and I take to the country road and head north back towards Louisburgh. Not much to report on our return inland journey but we are feeling the effect of two days marathon running. When we get to Killadoon we decide to walk a little. A car stops and the friendly driver offers us a lift. Of course, we refuse. I should emphasise to the *'Coastal Audit Committee'* that at no stage on this epic run have I ever accepted a lift from any individual in any type of moving apparatus!

We start running again. We are so glad to arrive in Louisburgh. Later in the evening Donald and I enjoy another delicious meal, followed by a brief visit to Matt Molloy's pub in Westport and a night-cap in the hotel bar.

Stage 67: Revisited: Friday 3 June 2022: Uggool, The Lost Valley (no extra mileage)

I did discover that in 1971, seventy-four people walked along here (from Thallabawn to Bundorragha). At the time there was talk of building a coastal road here and there were even plans drawn up in 1968 by Mayo Co. Council. The walk was like a campaign to promote the new coastal road, which was never built.

However, today I was able to revisit this area with Maureen and Brian with a bonus of getting a local guide to talk about the history of the area. Tours are given by Gerard Bourke, son of the late Michael who was on the 1971 walk. Today we walk on a *'green road'* that took us all the way from Bourkes house at Silver Strand through their farm at Uggool, now known as The Lost Valley. The tour took us as far as Killary Harbour, back down to Uggool beach and ends in the cottage from which Gerard's great-great-great grandfather, Pat Burke, was evicted in 1851.

At the Lost valley of Uggool

What an interesting and educational experience it was. I have to admit though I was disappointed originally, not to be allowed run along this beach back in March. The Bourkes have a strictly private property policy on their land. It's a pity that there isn't public access as I can't imagine too many people would ramble along in this area or cause any damage.

STAGE 68

Louisburg, Co. Mayo to Leenane, Co. Galway

Easter Saturday 16 April 2022

31.3 km or 19.4 miles

"My only want is that green grass, that lovely green grass - and you want to take it away from me" JB Keane, The Field

I'm mainly running on my own this weekend, but my support team, Maureen and Brian have joined me. They are going to walk part of the first stage with me along the infamous *famine road'* from Louisburgh to Delphi. We drove down from Bangor yesterday (Good Friday) and had the pleasure of staying with Maureen's cousins, Collette, and Bartley O'Malley. The O'Malley sheep farm has the perfect rural location in Laghta Eighter about 6km SE of Louisburgh and we are lucky to have a beautiful sight to wake up to, seeing Croagh Patrick from our bedroom.

Just before we leave the farm, we hear the lovely sound of the cuckoo. It's the first of the season but one of over 4,000 who will migrate from Africa to Ireland. We are delighted that Collette has decided to join us for the 'walking' part of today's coastal run. We arrange to leave one car at the Doolough Famine Memorial and drive back to Louisburg to begin today's adventure.

Today we are really re-enacting a famous but tragic event in Ireland's history: <u>The Doolough Famine Walk</u>

On 30 March 1849 during the Irish Famine a large body of starving people gathered in Louisburgh seeking food donations from the relieving officer. The officer didn't have 'his books' with him in Louisburgh so he informed the hungry locals that they would have to apply for food on the following day. However, the next day, officials had moved onto Delphi Lodge, ten miles away and that was where donations would be made available. So, in the morning, a procession of men, women and children made their way on foot across the 16 km mountain route to Delphi.

When the families arrived in Delphi, food was not forthcoming and they had to make their way back to Louisburgh again, tired, and hungry. On the return journey many died. Seven bodies were discovered the next morning and nine other people never returned home.

Every year there is an annual charity walk in May along the Louisburgh-Delphi route to commemorate those who suffered and perished. The walk also draws attention to human-rights abuses around the world. Archbishop Desmond Tutu, Chernobyl children and Kim Phúc (famously photographed as a girl running naked during the Vietnam War) are among those who have walked the walk. There are two memorials of the famine on the road – one a simple stone and the other quoting Mahatma Gandhi. *'How can men feel themselves honoured by the humiliation of their fellow beings'*

However, there is an uplifting connection between those who perished in Ireland and a Native American Tribe who suffered a similar fate around the same time; sixteen years previously in 1833, 20,000 people from the tribe of Choctaw were forced to walk their own 500-mile Trail of Tears to new land in Oklahoma. Thousands died on the way and more perished while struggling to set up homes in the new *'Indian Territory'*. Yet despite their own suffering, Choctaw Elders somehow received word in 1849 that people were starving to death in Ireland. The native tribe were able to collect US$170 to send to Ireland for famine relief - an amazing gesture on their behalf!

More than 170 years later, Ireland has rightly repaid the debt, helping to raise more than two million dollars for Native American tribes and nations which have been hardest hit by the coronavirus pandemic. An article in the 'New York Times' described the repayment perfectly, *'Irish return an old favor'*. The Choctaw word for a selfless act is *'iyyikowa'* it means serving those in need and the Irish word is *'neamhleithleasach'*.

Colette, Maureen & Brian walking towards Doolough on the famine road

As we're walking along the Doolough road, we can only imagine what a horrific journey this must have been for our starving ancestors. At least today we have a modern road to walk on, that conveniently cuts through the narrow valley.

Having said all that, it's still a long walk for Collette, Maureen, Brian, and me. It was 13.2km (or 8.2 miles) from Louisburg to the Doolough Memorials against a very strong southerly wind. At least the rain held off! As we arrive at the beautiful Doolough valley the mountains are towering above us. Ben Lugmore (803metres) and Mweelrea (814m) are on one side and Barrclashcame (772m) is on the other. All three peaks are higher than Croagh Patrick (764m). Doolough (black lake) also takes up most of the valley so in 1849 it would have been a treacherous, wet, and boggy route through the hills.

Maureen, Brian, and Collette drive back north to Louisburg and I begin running south along the narrow road with the lake on my right-hand side (Doolough Pass Road). I reach Killary Harbour, Ireland's only fjord and head east along the main road until I come to Aasleagh Falls. This is where the Erriff River reaches the sea at Killary. Just south of the Falls I see the sign *'Welcome to Co. Galway'*.

It's great to finally reach my native county and I'll be following the Connemara (west Galway) coast for the next few months. I can now see the mountain, Devils Mother in front of me. (Strangely the Irish name for it is ***Magairli an Deamhain'*** which translates as the 'demon's testicles'!).

Finally, I reach my finish line for today, the village of Leenane. It is perfect timing as Maureen and Brian arrive shortly and we head straight for ***'The Field'*** pub which became famous in the 1990 film. It is busy inside but we're lucky to find a cosy spot in the corner. Outside, the rain, that has been threatening for a while, pours down.

STAGE 69

Co. Galway: Leenane to Tully Cross

Easter Sunday 17 April 2022

34.4 km or 21.4 miles

"If people never did silly things, nothing intelligent would ever get done."
- Ludwig Wittgenstein

Once again for practical reasons I've decided to tackle this stage by running clockwise with the sea on my left. Maureen, Brian, and I stayed in Tully Cross in the *'Maol Reidh'* called after Connacht's highest mountain. Tony, the manager of the hotel welcomes us and when he hears my story, he donates a night's accommodation (plus an evening meal).

Today was one of those days where things seemed to go from bad to worse for me. For a start my hip has been giving me grief since Wednesday and yesterday's walk and run hasn't helped. Then I decided to have some porridge and poached eggs for breakfast. Not a great combination if you're going on a long run! Thirdly I was given wrong directions by a young man in the village. I asked him the way to Lettergesh Beach, and he sent me down towards Tully village. I had covered 4.5km before I arrived back at the hotel where I started my run, half an hour earlier!

When you're lost and this is the only person you meet!

Then finally after getting on the correct road, I followed a sign that said 'Beach' that I thought (wrongly!) would bring me down to Lettergesh Strand. I should point out that a lot of people reading this would have heard of Lettergesh as it was used in the famous horse racing scene in the 1952 film, *'The Quiet Man'*. Anyway, as I was running down this long narrow lane, I was thinking to myself, there is no way John Ford, and his production crew came along here.

My suspicions were correct and there wasn't even much of a beach at the end of the lane. I then struggled along the rocky and slippery coast as the rain was coming down. It was a miracle that I didn't fall over at some stage along here. I eventually I made my way back onto the country road and after a few miles I saw a clear sign pointing down to Lettergesh Beach.

Lettergesh beach where Quiet Man horserace was filmed

Yes, this beach was worth waiting for. Strangely Lettergesh is not named on the Ordnance Survey map, but it is on 'Google Maps'. It's divided into three parts and best to get here at low tide as I managed to do (my only bit of luck so far today!). Otherwise, you might not be able to get around the first section. As I was running along the strand, I was thinking that nothing has changed in the seventy years since they made *'The Quiet Man'*. The beautiful beach, the countryside and surrounding hills are exactly the same. They could still remake the horse racing scene today.

The rain is coming down again but I'm able to continue along the shoreline across a few fields before eventually reaching another wonderful beach, Glassillaun. From the car park here, I come to the T junction and take a left turn. I hope I'm going the right way but worry that this narrow boreen is going to come to a dead end. Luckily for me the lane conveniently hugs the coast around what's called, *'Killary Bay Little'*

I continue all the way down to the fishing harbour at Rosroe Pier. A good variety of fish are caught here, some I've never heard of before, such as pollock, wrasse, conger, ray, skate, shark, flounder, dabs, and dogfish. There is a Youth Hostel on the pier and a group seem to be going on a scuba diving expedition. A heavy shower pours down but I'm able to shelter in the hostel. I'm now at the very edge of Killary Harbour, just opposite the Lost Valley of Uggool on the other side.

The famous philosopher Ludwig Wittgenstein, a former soldier who survived WW1, lived in this remote area in 1948. The Austrian wanted a simple life in Killary. He found peace and a fascination with nature here under the shadow of Mweelrea where he could put his thoughts together. ***"We are asleep. Our life is a dream, but we wake up sometimes, just enough to know that we are dreaming."***

Just up from Rosroe Pier is a signposted walk. I spotted it as a dotted line on the OS map and I know I can follow it all the way along the southern shore of Killary Harbour. It is rough going at the beginning, impossible to run on and the path sometimes disappears. It is also quite a dangerous trail in parts (especially on a wet day like today) with steep descents down to the narrow fjord. I read that this trail is called a *'famine relief'* road. I think that means that it was built for no other reason than to justify rewarding the local hungry people in the area, making sure they did something to 'earn' their payment This was a common occurrence during the famine; building roads or walls that served no purpose.

I spot lots of large shellfish beds below me in Killary Harbour. Soon the trail improves and I'm able to run again. Shortly I meet a jolly group of about fifteen walkers. They are called the *'Wayfarers'* and they're a Dublin-based hiking and mountaineering club.

Wayfarers Hiking Group at Killary Harbour coastal path

Eventually the rough path that I'm running on turns into a much easier country road which I follow all the way until it joins up with the N59. The sign on the main road says, Leenane 7km. It's mostly downhill towards my finish line but just as I'm feeling smug and confident, the sky darkens, and the rain comes down again.

This time it's more than just a shower. It's relentless for about half an hour and I arrive in Leenane soaked to the skin. I'm so glad to see Maureen and Brian and I enjoy a tasty bowl of seafood chowder. After lunch we go to the Forge Craft Shop and Maureen buys me an Aran sweater. Hot soup and a warm Aran jumper, just what the doctor ordered!

STAGE 70

Co. Galway: Tully Cross to Cleggan

Saturday 21 May 2022

43.6 km or 27.1 miles

'Our friends go with us as we go down the long path where beauty winds, so why should we fear to join our friends'. Oliver St John Gogarty

We've returned to the lovely village of Tully Cross in Connemara and the plan for this weekend is to reach Clifden, the largest town in this area. Since my last run I also completed the Belfast marathon. This was my third (and probably last ever marathon!) and I struggled again trying to get under four hours

It's an early morning for me at the beautiful Maol Reidh Hotel. I grab some fruit, cereal and a nice mug of coffee before hitting the road at 7.20am. Before the village of Tully, I take a loop that brings me down to the pier. I have to climb over a few fences but shortly I come to a sandy beach (White Strand) at *'Island View'*

Out in the bay I see Crump Island (Oilean De Chruinne). I read that St. Patrick's nephew, Rioch had a small chapel on the island. Also, there seems to be a dispute as to which county Crump Island belongs to. Those greedy Mayo people have tried to claim it as their own but as a proud Galwegian I'll argue that the island is one of ours.

Across a few more fields and I reach Renvyle House which is now a hotel. It was originally owned by the Blake family who were not the most popular of landlords. In the 1880's, as a protest, some tenants drove their cattle onto the Blake's land. This was common practice at the time and in 1916 my own grandfather was involved in a similar protest and spent twelve weeks in Galway jail for *'cattle driving'.*

In the 1920's Renvyle House was bought by Oliver St. John Gogarty (writer, surgeon, and senator). His love affair with Connemara began when he lost his heart to a Galway girl (just like me!).

I like the way Gogarty describes the location of Renvyle House

'My house stands on a lake, but it stands also on the sea - waterlilies meet the golden seaweed. Behind me, islands and the mountainous mainland share in a final reconciliation, at this, the world's end.'

I'm able to run between the gap of the sea and the lake (Rusheenduff Lough) and along a lovely grassy path as Gogarty says, where 'waterlilies meet the golden seaweed'

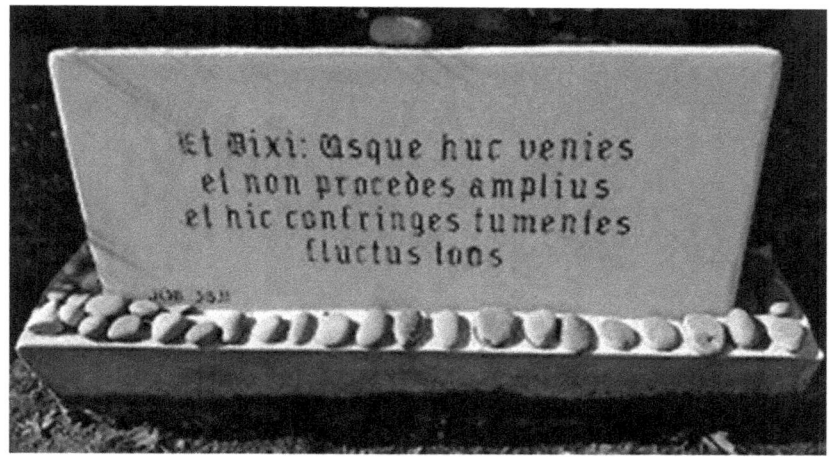

Speaking of writing, there's a biblical inscription on a paved stone by the shore behind Renvyle House. Maybe it was best I wasn't able to translate it at the time, because it says, *'this far you may come and no further; here is where your proud waves halt'.* This quotation is part of the text in the Bible where Job is wondering how the tides behave. The tides continue to fascinate me and as I run along the coast, I'm always amazed how the coastal landscape can change twice a day, every day.

After looping around Rusheenduff lake, I join up with the country road again. I pass Renvyle Castle where the pirate queen Grace O'Malley (Granuaile) made her home when she married Donal O'Flaherty in 1546. (one of her three husbands). Nearby is the *'Church*

of the Seven Daughters' built by an Omey Island chief in thanks for cures that his daughters received from a local holy well. I continue west all the way to Renvyle Point. My plan is to run around Tully Mountain by the coast which turns out to be quite a difficult task with lots of rough terrain and many fences to climb over (both barbed wire and electric).

I was lucky to avoid a stampede of cows who came marching towards me, probably thinking I had their breakfast. I sprinted away and even received a slight shock after jumping over an electric fence but at least I knew the cattle couldn't follow me!

Circling around Tully Mountain

Going around Tully Mountain was a lonely stretch of the coast. Oscar Wilde referred to the ***'savage beauty of Connemara'*** and I know exactly what he means. For miles all I could hear was a squawking bird, maybe it was wondering what this strange two-legged creature was doing in its territory. It was probably a raven or maybe it was the famous bald eagle, Maol Reidh, that Connacht's highest mountain is named after. I spotted quite a few hares too, some of them the size of small dogs and of course lots of sheep clambering to the edge of Tully Mountain. There were lovely views here with Inishbroon Island stretching out to the north and Braadillaun Island almost connected to the coast.

Eventually I reached a small farm where sheep were bleating like crazy. After clambering over a few more fences, I arrived at Letter Beag where the farmers track begins its descent to Letterfrack. Diamond Hill (442 metres high) now dominates the skyline as I start to circle around Ballynakill Harbour. Soon I arrive in Letterfrack where I have a short break at Kebo Café. I continue and stay south of Loch an Gheafra Bhain and then follow the road which takes me all the way to Ross Beach. There are lovely views of sandy Freaghillaun Island from here and way out in the distance I can clearly see Inishbofin Island. (Island of the white cow)

Shiny stones on Ross Beach

With no more roads or tracks along here I struggle through the rough terrain. At this stage all my energy had disappeared, and I knew I wouldn't reach Cleggan Cliffs today, so just east of Ballynew beach I followed an inland trail that brought me back to the road just north of Ballynakill Lough. One last kilometre takes me to Cleggan Harbour (another one of Nimmo's piers). It's been a tough day but I'm so glad to see Maureen and Brian there to greet me.

Stage 70- Revisited: Saturday 13 August 2022 Cleggan Cliffs, Co. Galway: 11.4 km or 7.1 miles.

Today I returned to complete this stage on one of hottest days of the year. At Cleggan I drove across the slipway (between the sea and the lagoon) and then took a narrow road to the left. I followed the boreen that turned into a track and then jogged along a perfect grassy track, keeping Cleggan Bay on my left.

I decided to leave the trail and headed directly towards Cleggan Head, making sure to cover the western corner at the top of the peninsula. I'm now fifty metres above sea level and have a nice view of Inishbofin and Inishshark.

Cleggan Head

A lone boatman breaks the silence as he heads out to sea on such a beautiful morning. I loop around the coast eastwards and re-join the grassy track.

The coast seems to zig zag over the next couple of miles. I see a couple of people in the distance which is rare but always a good sign as they must have taken some road or trail to get here. I strike up a conversation with the couple who come from Germany. Their English isn't very good and even though I've spent time in Germany, my basic German makes it a fairly short conversation.

The good news is that I can now follow a narrow trail that will bring me all the way back to the main road. On the way I take a detour down to Ballynew Beach. This was as far as I reached on 21st May, so I'm now satisfied I've completed the whole peninsula.

Lovely surprise bumping into Michael Stitt, just outside Cleggan

I have almost completed my loop when a car passes me and beeps. I can hear someone shout out the window, *'Gerry, Gerry'*. I'm wondering who even knows I'm here in the wilds of Connemara! It turns out to be Michael Stitt, a colleague from North Down AC who just happened to be holidaying in the area with his son, James. It was a lovely surprise to meet them both just as I was finishing today's circular run.

STAGE 71

Co. Galway: Cleggan to Clifden

Sunday 22 May 2022

24.0 km or 14.9 miles

'A shoulder of rock sticks high up out of the sea, A fisherman's mark for lobster and blue shark' Richard Murphy describing High Island

Last night Maureen, Brian and I stayed in the Ocean Wave B&B just west of Salerno Beach, near Cleggan. I'm now in the townland known as Rossadillask which has suffered a lot in the last 175 years. Stories of the famine in this area are appalling. I was reading a horrific report about how children were suffering from dysentery and a mother was struggling to keep her son alive *'all the medicine he wanted was food'*, she said. In October 1927 another disaster hit the area when a sudden storm caused the death of twenty-six fishermen in this area.

This morning I'm lucky that it's low tide. Not only can I reach the island of Gooreen but the whole area is brightening up with silver beaches everywhere, one after the other. No wonder the sign on the road said, *'You are now entering Rossadillask, Paradise'*. Even though there is little sunshine, the area has a bright sunny appearance.

I knew the next part of my adventure would be tricky. I was attempting to reach the other side of Lough Atalia Bay. Even with the low tide I still needed to cross two wide streams. In one section of the stream, right in the middle, I spotted a small boat. I was then able to wade up to my knees and complete the crossing in two stages, using the boat to manoeuvre my way to the other side.

Near Rossadillask (or 'Paradise' as its sometimes called)

I come to Anchor beach, called after the anchor that is still very visible today. It's part of the wreck of the *'Verity'* that crashed here in 1890. Further inland is Aughrusbeg Lough, and I follow the road around the lake. Out on the Atlantic, I can see Friar Island and behind that is High Island.

Anchor from wreck of Verity on Anchor Beach

St. Fechin founded a monastery here in 634 and St Gormgal lived on High Island in the year 1000 (the first millennium). It was around this time that Brian Boru, the high King of Ireland, came here for his confession. Shortly after this, King Brian won a famous battle in Clontarf in 1014.

I shortly arrive near Sweeneys Pub at Claddaghduff. It's only 9.00am and probably too early for a drink! It's much quieter than I expected, and I even get a glimpse of the famous Sky Road on the other side of the bay as I get closer to Clifden.

However, once I reach the junction and join the N59 it becomes quite busy. If I had more time (and energy) I would have taken the Sky Road loop and entered Clifden, that way which would have made a lot more sense. (I'll be back to do the Sky Road again) Today I'm happy to arrive at my destination at 10.30am and I enjoy my coffee and cream doughnut. It's been another tough challenge this weekend but I'm happy to finally reach Clifden, the capital of Connemara.

Stage 71: Revisited: Omey Island: Saturday 16 September 2023: 11.0 km or 6.8 miles

'Now morn has come and with the morn the punctual tide again'. Susan Coolidge

Strava map showing my run around Omey Island

I had to revisit Omey Island as I missed it in May 2022 on my original coastal run. Today I was privileged to have my sister-in-law Aideen Hurley with me and once again Maureen and Brian joined me. We owe a lot to Aideen and her husband Kieran. We've stayed so many times at their beautiful house in Oranmore and it has been a great base for me on the Co. Galway section of the coastal run. Low tide is at 2.00pm so we had plenty of time to get here from Galway city. It's such an amazing site to see the huge expanse of open sand that fills up and drains away, twice a day. This island has a magic of its own that never disappoints me.

Getting ready to go across to Omey Island

Omey is a unique place and has been special for me for almost fifty years and even before I ever set foot on the island. I discovered this tidal island through reading Walter Macken's most famous book *'Rain on the Wind'* where the main character spends time in Connemara. My passion for Omey and for Macken's book has even led me to even writing a play *'Island of Saints & Skeletons'*.

Here in Omey the islanders were really the last pagans in Ireland, and this was over 200 years after St Patrick arrived. Patrick never made it this far west and years later Saint Fechin was bequeathed Omey Island from the king of Connacht. However, nobody told the Omey natives that Saint Fechin was the owner of the island, and they didn't take too well to him trying to convert them.

Anyway, back to today. About halfway across the strand I leave Maureen, Brian and Aideen and start running. I stick to the road markers on the beach. Don't forget you can drive across to Omey Island. It is quite safe, except at the hours close to high tide. When

I arrive on Omey itself, I run along the lane that loops around the southern section of the island.

Declan with his herd of cattle on Omey Island

The narrow road takes me to the southern corner of the island and just before I reach the end, I spot a farmer in front of me herding cattle. His name is Declan, and he tells me he is a native of Omey Island but has now moved to the mainland. The sun was shining as we talked, and Declan pointed out all the other Connemara islands in front of us, Inishturk (not to be confused with the Co. Mayo island of the same name), an Chruach Island, Friar Island and High Island.

I told Declan about my bad experience with cows, but he assured me that his cows were the friendliest ones as they were used to people being around. We talked about Omey and the *'Hillock na Mna'*, the ancient burial hill where only women were buried. Three hundred female bones were excavated there. Declan told me exactly where the hill was, so I made sure to climb to the top later.

Later, when I did reach the top of the 'Hillock of the Women' I had a great view all over Connemara. Looking down on Omey strand I spotted two figures way in the distance. It looked like Maureen and Brian, so I phoned Maureen and we waved to each other across the island.

I passed Omey's ancient graveyard which is still used today. Funerals at nearby Claddaghduff Church must match the low tides before the mourners can go to the cemetery. I decide to take a longer route back. I cross the wide strand and keep running south towards *'Cnoc an Bhiora'* on the mainland. I leave the shore, climb up a small cliff but suddenly I arrive right in the middle of someone's back garden.

I apologise to a couple who are enjoying the late summer weather. Lucky for me, they are very friendly, offering tea and chatting away. I might have stayed longer but I knew Maureen, Brian and Aideen were waiting for me at Sweeney's Pub. I said goodbye and join the road in front of their house. This detour added another 2k to my journey back to Claddaghduff - but all in all, today was one of my favourite runs of my coastal adventure. Yes, as an American archaeologist once said, Omey Island is indeed *'the most beautiful, gentle, sweet place'*.

STAGE 72

Co. Galway: Clifden to Ballyconneely

Saturday 4 June 2022

42.6 km or 26.5 miles

'And he knows that he'll regret the leaving, knows that he will pine for grieving, for the sky road by the singing sea'.  *(Song by Frances Black)*

It's a beautiful morning in Connemara and I feel privileged to be running in such a lovely area on such a perfect day. Carmel at *'Teach an Easard'*, where we're staying, has left out cereal and fruit for me and I begin my run at 6.15am in glorious sunshine.

As I run along the coast the only person, I see is a lady going in for a swim at Coral Strand just outside Ballyconneely. I take a left at Derryeighter and loop around this peninsula, heading west with the sun behind me. The road veers north of Lough Usk and south of Loch an tSaile (another salty lagoon). It's still only 7.00am and so quiet here but suddenly I hear a cuckoo, probably over from Africa and enjoying our beautiful, but cooler weather.

On the way back to the R341 it's surprisingly hilly and I can see in the distance the Alcock & Brown airplane monument.

Alcock & Brown Monument

This is one of two monuments commemorating the first ever non-stop transatlantic crossing in 1919. I run down the hill from the first memorial, join the R341 and cross to the second site.

This area doubles up to commemorate two historical firsts, crossing the Atlantic by Alcock & Brown and remembering Guglielmo Marconi who transmitted wireless messages across the Atlantic.

In 1919 British aviators Alcock and Brown both dreamed of achieving the first non-stop transatlantic flight! They left from Newfoundland and after a long 16-hour flight they finally spotted land. The plane was damaged on arrival due to a precarious landing, in what appeared to be a suitable field, but turned out to be a bog. They touched down on Irish soil on June 15, 1919.

Coincidentally, the land where the plane crashed was owned by Marconi for his own transatlantic transmissions. I can only imagine what a risky and scary adventure Alcock

& Brown had during those sixteen hours over the Atlantic. Unfortunately, Alcock was killed, just six months later, when he crashed near Rouen as part of the Paris Air show.

I think I can say that Maureen and I (and our son, Conor) have a connection to this historical event. We previously visited this site in 1994 on 15 June which was exactly 75 years after the landing. We then met 82-year-old Harry Sullivan who, as a seven-year-old in 1919, witnessed the flight coming in near Clifden.

1994 Photo with Maureen & our son, Conor, and Harry Sullivan (the man who actually saw the plane coming in over the Atlantic in 1919)

Harry describes the plane coming in, *'Its huge wings nearly touched the top of the church. I watched as it roared away towards the bog, its wings swaying up and down'.*

I continue running towards Clifden. It's quite a crooked road and I need to be careful around every bend. I finished my bottle of water that I had planted at the Marconi site the day before (the old ultra-runner's trick!) but I'm feeling thirsty again and need a break. In Clifden, I stop at a cafe for water, coffee, and a croissant. After about ten minutes I continue and take the beach road along the shore and follow the sign for the *'Sky Road'*.

I spot a lone Connemara Pony grazing in a field. I had heard that the unique breed of horse evolved from stallions that swam ashore at Slyne Head after a ship wreck around 1820. Others say the breed of Pony arrived earlier than that from one of the many Spanish Armada ships that crashed off the west coast in 1588. Out in the sea I see a big white marker that looks like a Lighthouse. It's actually a daytime marker to help navigate boats. Locally, it's nicknamed the *'White Lady'.*

I'm almost at the top of the long climb up the Sky Road when I hear a car beep behind me. It's Maureen and Brian. They have enjoyed their full breakfast at 'Teach an Easard' in Ballyconneely and have caught up with me.

I continue running and we arrange to meet a few miles further west at Eyrephort beach. (Iar Phoirt). It's a lovely downhill run for me and my fastest kilometre of the day (5.04 mins). At Eyrephort beach we reunite. It's warmer here, the sea is turquoise (or Caribbean blue) and it's the most perfect place for a picnic. Interestingly, Eyrephort is one of only three places in Ireland where there is evidence of Viking graves. The other two sites are in Arklow and in Ballyholme Beach, Bangor, just a stone's throw from where I live.

Brian & Maureen on Eyrephort Beach with Inishturk behind

We linger here for a good two hours in this secluded spot protected by the surrounding islands of Omey, Inishturk and Turbot. Reluctantly, I leave the tropical beach and I continue running along the north shore of the Sky Road as far as the main junction. Maureen picks me up there and afterwards in Clifden we enjoy a relaxing lunch, sitting outside in perfect warm sunshine.

STAGE 73

Co. Galway: Ballyconneely Peninsula loop

Thursday 2 June 2022

24.4 km or 15.2 miles

'Oh man, seek out the fair land under the Beanna Beola and you will be free',
Walter Macken

For practical reasons I decided to complete this section before Stage 72. Maureen, Brian, and I drive out from Galway City, passing through Maam Cross and then suddenly the hills of Connemara open up in front of us. The mountains are known as the *'Twelve Pins'* or Na Beanna Beola and, although I've been here many times before, there's still something magical and mysterious about them. The sky is brightening up and we see no rain at all for the rest of the weekend.

Maureen drops me off just north of Ballyconneely, beside the Connemara Sands Hotel on Mannin Bay. I stay on the country road for a while and then make my way down through the lush green fields to the German sounding beach, Traumstrand (dream strand). I stick to the shore, running along another dreamy strand. This one is called Tra Fada (long beach) and takes me all the way to Knock Hill. The terrain is rougher up here but as I descend there are lots of lovely sand dunes to run through. Shortly I come to a beautiful beach at Doonloughan.

So far, it's been perfect running territory along the strands and soft sandy grass. Suddenly though just before I reach Doonloughan Pier the shoreline becomes very rocky, and I struggle for a while over wobbly boulders and seaweed. I follow the country road inland and after about 3km I take a right turn along a rough boreen. I might not have spotted this turn if I didn't meet a lady at her house who kindly gave me a bottle of water too. She assured me that a narrow country lane would lead me through Connemara Golf Course and the shore on the south side of the peninsula.

I run through a couple of fields and meet a group of horse riders along here, near the aptly named *'Horse Island'*. I'm struggling now and envy those horses with their four long legs. The shore becomes rocky but I'm able to run along a grassy path for a while before climbing a gate and reaching Bunowen (foot of the river).

I stick to the road for the rest of the run into Ballyconneely, passing Doon Hill which was once an extinct volcano. The watch station at the top of the hill was manned in both World Wars to check on any possible enemy invasion.

I carry on running towards Ballyconneely and I have a nice surprise as I realise that I'm running on the road where our guest house is (Teach an Easard). It's about a mile outside the village. Maureen and Brian have just arrived at the B&B so it's a perfect ending to today's adventure.

Stage 73- Revisited: Saturday 13 August 2022 Slyne Head, Co. Galway: 9.1 km or 5.7 miles

When I initially did Stage 73 on 2nd June, I had come along a boreen from Doonloughan Bay that brought me to the Golf Club, but I hadn't reached the SW corner of this peninsula. So today I felt I needed to get closer to Slyne Head, which is on the western tip of a group of islands. The most westerly island is called Illaunamid (Oilean Imill or Wood Island) and this is where two Slyne lighthouses are situated.

Connemara in all its glory with twelve pins in distance

Today was extremely warm and I had already run around Cleggan Cliffs (another re-visitation!) earlier in the morning. I then drove to this area and parked my car just before the Golf Course and started my run (or walk) at 11.33am. ***'Mad dogs and Irishmen'*** might have been an apt phrase for me today in the Connemara midday sun! Even on a perfect Saturday in warm sunshine, like today, there were only a few people around. At the caravan park I had to climb up from the strand to get around a rocky and tricky cliff section. Eventually I reached the SW corner of the peninsula. The beach here was completely deserted. As I got closer to Slyne Head I met a couple who had been snorkeling nearby. They were Eimear and Pat Irwin from Belmullet.

Soon I could see the lighthouses on Slyne Head. Both were built in 1836 but only one of them is now in use. Since I've started this whole adventure in 2017 this is the most westerly point I've reached. I can hardly feel a breeze, even though I'm now surrounded on all sides by the Atlantic Ocean.

The Vikings from Iceland were regular visitors to this area and in fact it was a shorter journey for them to get to Slyne Head, compared to the longer distance from Iceland to Scandinavia. As well as being strong oarsmen, the Viking boats had a large sail made from wool that allowed the boat to move as quickly as sixteen miles per hour. They even had their own name for Slyne Head, calling it Jolduhlaup.

STAGE 74

Co. Galway: Ballyconneely to Roundstone

Thursday 29 September 2022

22.7 km or 14.1 miles

"Sometimes the most scenic roads in life are the detours you didn't mean to take." (Sign outside Coffee Cottage in Roundstone)

We stayed in a lovely B&B (Island View) in Roundstone on the Thursday night with the perfect host in Maurice. Also, two weeks ago, I *'pre-visited'* this area and completed both Inis Nee Island and the Rosroe Peninsula (in perfect weather) which made it easier for me over these days.

For the first few miles I ran along the main R341, taking a right at Murvey. I probably could have taken an earlier turn at Callow that would have brought me down to the shore, but I wasn't sure of the terrain there. On the coast road I met a father and son who were building a wall, making the most of the fine weather. The man pointed out for me the island of Croaghnakeela although he called it Deer Island as it was once stocked with deer. I left the working men, and I was able to rough it for about half a mile over a rocky hill before reaching another trail. As I climbed over a small summit, I could see this beautiful beach in front of me. It was Dogs Bay beach (Tra Chuan na Mhada) in all its glory.

I followed the proper trail back up to the main road and had the perfect downhill run to Dogs Bay or Tra Mhantan. (Mantan was an apostle of Saint Patrick). When I reached the beautiful beach, I kept running, even meeting along the way a French ultra-runner, Michel Le Merle, and his wife Janet.

Gorteen Bay: The other side of Dogs Bay

This looped run was tougher than I expected with lots of boulders on the southern part of the peninsula to manoeuvre around. However, the rewards at the other end when I eventually reached Gorteen Bay (Port na Feadoige) were more than worth it. Such a spectacular crescent shaped beach with the perfect white sand and clear blue water. To cap it all, Maureen and Brian were there to meet me.

I thought I could make it along the shore all the way to Roundstone, but the surface got much too difficult. I think if I had persevered a little more past Ervallagh I could have made it the whole way and joined up with a coastal trail. Instead, I ran up the boreen to the main road that took me to my destination for today

Cloch Na Ron and Bruce Ismay

The name Roundstone is a bad English translation and I much prefer the prettier sounding Irish name, *'Cloch Na Ron'* (Rock of the Seals). It's said that Bruce Ismay, chairman of the White Star Line (owners of Titanic) came here in 1912 for some peace. I figure he could not have been very popular after surviving the voyage by getting onto one of the lifeboats.

STAGE 75

Co. Galway: Roundstone to Glynsk

Friday 30 September 2022

28.1 km or 17.5 miles

*"I can only think in the dark and in Connemara
I have found the last pool of darkness in Europe."*
(From Tim Robinson's book, The Last Pool of Darkness)

I almost cancelled today's run! Hurricane Ian in Florida has destroyed a lot of property in the US and according to the RTE Weather Forecast the storm is coming to the west of Ireland, with torrential rainfall and strong winds. And yes, it did rain a lot during the night, and it was quite blustery in the morning.

It's 8.00 am, dark and wet as I start this morning's run. After about 3km I passed the bridge to the island of Inishnee. In hindsight it was such a good decision to complete this island two weeks ago when the weather was much better (see later). Despite the miserable rain today I was also lucky to have a strong west wind behind me.

Inspiration sign in Roundstone

I followed the main road and head south towards Aillenacally. The old village contains fourteen houses now deserted and in disrepair. Years ago, schoolchildren used to walk from here in a north direction through the bog to the school at Toombeola. There were steppingstones to guide you across the path. It was called *'The Scholars' Road'*. According to local writer Michael Halliday, the walk or trail starts about 400 metres up from the shore but it's still difficult to find. Luckily for me, I met a local farmer at the exact spot where the steppingstones began. At this stage it was pouring rain, but I was able to make my way across the bog, trying to find the odd stone to step on. Sometimes it was so boggy and wet that I had to leave the path for a dryer section. All the time I was thinking of those poor children on cold and wet mornings taking this same journey. About two thirds of the way across I did lose the trail. The stones seemed to disappear, so I had to plod along through the fields. Eventually I could see houses nearby and I was able to climb over a farmgate to reach the main road at Toombeola. The literal translation is *'Tomb of Beola'*. Beola was an ancient chief in Connemara.

Shortly I cross over a bridge and then take a right turn signposted to Cashel. This section of the road is quite narrow and winds its way around the shore. I'm reminded of how Tim Robinson described it *'the road has to swerve and twist like a cyclist chased by a snappy sheepdog'*. Robinson was a Yorkshire writer who like the Normans 'became more Irish than the Irish themselves'. I passed by the entrance to Rosroe Peninsula and count myself lucky that I've already completed that section of the coast (see later) in much better weather.

I decided to have a break at Cashel House Hotel and hopefully get some water to drink. All that rain and I'm still thirsty! The sign outside the hotel said 'Residents Only' but I ventured inside. A young lady gave me a big jug of water and I sat in the lobby knocking back a few glasses. Back in 1969 Charles de Gaulle, just a month after his resignation as president of France, came to Ireland, and spent two weeks here at the hotel. Cashel House only received a week's notice that the big man was coming. There was great panic as management worried, they did not have a bed big enough for the six-foot five inches (1.96 metres) Frenchman. I like the comment in the Irish Times at the time that has a connection to my adopted town in Northern Ireland.

> *'The presence of General de Gaulle here is almost as bizarre as would be the announcement that Chairman Mao had arrived in Bangor, Co Down, to enjoy the amenities of Pickie Pool.'*

At the time De Gaulle tried to explain why he came here. *'It was a sort of instinct that led me towards Ireland, perhaps because of the Irish blood that courses in my veins.'* There was some truth in the president's comment about his Irish blood. His grandmother was descended from the McCartans of Co Down and she even wrote a book about Daniel O'Connell. The rain was still coming down as I left the hotel. I followed a narrow road on the peninsula to Lehenagh and then joined the main road all the way to my finish line in Glynsk.

I'm glad to have completed today's adventure as I have been feeling more tired recently. I think the two marathons (Manchester and Belfast) I did in the springtime took a lot out of me. Recently I got my bloods checked and I was diagnosed as being anemic with low iron levels. A second blood test later proved more positive, but I am realising I've got to eat more iron-based foods. That can be hard sometimes as I do not eat any red meat. Today at Glynsk House Maureen, Brian and I enjoyed delicious tea and scones, watching the sun making its first appearance of the day and brightening up those dark hills of Connemara.

Stage 75- PRE-visit: Saturday 17 September 2022 Rosroe Peninsula, Cashel. 16.0 km or 9.9 miles

As I drove out from Galway City, I watched the early morning fog clear to reveal the peaks and valleys of the twelve pins (na Beanna Beola).

Rosroe Peninsula with na Beanna Beola behind

Rosroe translates as the *'the red peninsula'* and called after the boggy terrain. I couldn't find anything on-line about this area so maybe I am one of the few people to circumnavigate the Rosroe peninsula. It's so quiet and peaceful with perfect still water as I run along the southern shore of Cloonisle Bay (or Blackhaven Bay).

Standoff with cow near Canower Pier, Rosroe Peninsula

On the east side of the peninsula, I eventually found a rough and rocky trail that joined up with the country road near Rosroe Lodge. I then took a slight detour down to Canower Pier. On my way back a cow insists on blocking my way so I have to rough through some long grass before completing the Rosroe loop.

Stage 75- PRE-visit: Saturday 17 September 2022: Inis Nee Island 12.0 km or 7.5 miles

After completing Rosroe Peninsula (see above) I got into my car and headed west, taking a left turn, signposted Inis Ni, just before Roundstone. Even before a bridge was built, islanders could make their way across the rocks, to reach the mainland.

Roundstone itself is notoriously busy over the summer but, even on a beautiful Saturday like today, it's very quiet here in Inis Nee on the other side of village. I start my run and take an immediate left, passing a few houses. Eventually I do join up with a lane that brings me down to a pier and I'm able to cross over to the middle section of the island. I take a left turn which leads me onto the most beautiful grassy coastal path.

Inis Nee Island - the perfect coastal path!

This trail is perfect for running on and to cap it all, there are magnificent views of the Twelve Pins (na Beanna Beola). These mountains are spectacular today and watching over me wherever I am. I follow the road to the very end and do my own loop through the bog. I then double back the whole way and follow the straight road north all the way back to the bridge. Bye-bye, Inis Nee.

STAGE 76

Co. Galway: Glynsk to Cill Chiarain

Saturday 29 October 2022

31.7 km or 19.7 miles

'After Mass, the rain had drained away into a tide of sunlight on which we sailed out to St MacDara's Island and dipped our sails. Both of us smiling.' (Paul Durcan)

We returned to Glynsk House where I finished my run the last time. The big issue today and tomorrow was trying to avoid the heavy rain blowing in from the Atlantic Ocean. It poured all morning and it's still raining at noon as we leave Galway City. However, all changes when we reach Glynsk, and it turns out to be a beautiful day.

There is a rich history of music and songs in this part of Connemara and the famous musician Seamus Ennis collected tunes in this area and helped revive traditional music in the 1960's. His own specialty was the beautiful sounding, uilleann pipes and he even inspired groups like Planxty and the Bothy Band. It all started in 1942 when Seamus was employed by the Folklore Commission to visit Connemara to collect ancient tunes. He was given *'a pen, some paper and pushbike'*.

Unfortunately, I don't even have a pushbike today. I could have used one as I headed west from Glynsk along the quiet country roads.

Moyrus Cemetery (Reilig Mhairois)

I pass a memorial dedicated to four men who were drowned in February 1921. This was the time of the *'War of Independence'* and they were young volunteers making their way by boat to Roundstone. They perished after a violent storm around the island of Inishlacken.

Memorial to four young men drown at sea

Running along the beach I'm able to stay by the shore and follow a coastal track called *'Luibin Mhairois'* (The Moyrus Trail). There are even stiles and markers along here which you don't see very often on the Irish coast. However, after all the rain we've had over the last few weeks, it is very damp and muddy on this path. There are a few large boulders and it's hard to decide whether to clamber over the big rocks or to try to stay on the flooded grassy trail.

Moyruss Loop Walk: Always great when I see a stile

I'm really appreciating the lovely weather now and the beautiful views back towards the Maam Turks and the Beanna Beola (Twelve Pins). It's a perfect afternoon in the middle of a long weekend but I still don't meet anyone on the Moyruss Loop. In the distance I spot the Global Aerosol Watch station which is one of the longest running mercury recording stations in the world. The station's position in the countryside is important, away from neighbouring towns, to ensure that no pollutants interfere with recordings. I can vouch for the fact that this is indeed a very remote location.

I reach Dooyeher and I'm able to join a country road for a while as far as An Leathmhas (Halfmace) but then the boreen comes to a sudden end. I decide (in my wisdom) to rough it across a few wet fields and over some dreaded barbed wired fences as I know I can reach another lane. A Connemara pony is watching my every move and I'm trying to stay out of his territory. Along here I spot a row of deserted houses, a reminder of how previous families tried to make a living here, on the edge of the Atlantic.

This whole area has a strong history of emigration and it's interesting to point out that Marty Walsh, recent mayor of Boston has a strong connection to south Connemara. His father was from Carna and his mother was from Rosmuc. Mayor Walsh was the perfect person to open the Emigrant Commemorative Centre in Carna. Bonfires welcomed him home and signs said *'Fáilte Abhaile, Mayor Marty Walsh'*

I make my way across the damp fields to a harbour, Ceibh an Mhasa which is probably the nearest point to the popular MacDara's island. Saint MacDara is the patron saint of fishermen and there's even a special saint's day (and festival) devoted to him on 16 July every year. Locals say St MacDara's Day can feel like Christmas Day with so many people returning home to the area.

On this adventure around the Irish coast, I've referred so often to the many Spanish Armada ships that sunk in 1588. Remember, the Spanish were losing the *'Battle of Gravelines'* against the British Navy and decided to take the scenic route north from the English Channel. Two more of their ships went down off the Connemara coast. The *'Falco Blanco Mediano'* crashed just a few miles north of here, near Freaghillaun island and the *'Concepcion Del Cano'* sank here at the spot where I am now. This area is called *'Duirling na Spanneach'* *(rock bank of the Spaniards).*

Over three hundred Spanish sailors survived and Sir William Fitzwilliam, the Lord deputy of Ireland, gave orders that they be brought to Galway City to be executed. They were then taken to Forthill Cemetery. Three hundred Spanish sailors were then beheaded and presumably buried without any ceremony. There is a plaque in Forthill Cemetery near Galway docks with inscriptions in Irish and Spanish, remembering this terrible event.

It's starting to drizzle as I continue my run. When I finally reach the village of Carna, I stop to get water. I'm in the heart of the Gaeltacht now and I tell myself to make more of an effort to speak Irish. The rest of today's journey is straight forward as I continue east for eight kilometres on the main R340. The house we're staying at is called Aill na Brun, just about a mile west of Cill Chiarain. Maureen and Brian are already settling in when I arrive after completing today's run.

Stage 76 (Revisited): Co. Galway: Islands of Mweenish & Roisin na Chalaidh: Monday 31 October 2022: 13.4 km or 8.3 miles

'How lucky the young man who will have her to wed, the guiding star of the morning, and a torch in the evening' Padraic Ó Flatharta from Carna

It is a miserable morning here in south Connemara. No sign of the rain stopping, and the trick is to try to avoid the heavy showers. I sneak out of the house in Cill Chiarain at about 7.30 am and drive the five miles to Carna, parking my car at the big car park at Tigh Mheaic. Just as I'm ready to begin my run to the islands, the heavens open and torrential rain falls. I quickly retreat to my car and wait for it to subside.

First, I have to cross a causeway to the island of Roisin na Chalaidh. It's hard to believe that 53 people lived on this tiny island in 1841. I don't think the causeways were built until the 1890's so it would have been difficult for people then. With all the rain and floods, there is water everywhere, especially on Roisin na Chalaidh Island. It's hard to imagine anyone trying to make a living in this small space.

I keep running south and finally reach Mweenish Island. Six hundred and fifty people lived here in 1841. The islanders are famous for building **'Galway Hookers'** which were boats to carry turf even as far as the Burren in Co. Clare.

When I arrive in Mweenish more torrential rain starts falling. I spot a man on the road, and he welcomes me to stand in his shed until it stops. I run to the most westerly point on the island spotting Mason Island a few hundred metres across the sea. The island has been uninhabited since 1954. The writer, Liam O'Flaherty describes the last residents to leave Mason Island who probably embarked at this spot.

'When a frail canvas currach rode in from the Atlantic and touched ashore on the sandy beach at Mweenish, two figures, sixty years old Patrick Cloherty and his fifty-nine years old sister, Mary, arrived in a new and strange world.'

The 'strange world' they arrived on was here on Mweenish island but connected by bridge to the mainland. Patrick and Mary, both deaf since birth and had never previously left home. I also read how previous storms had washed over Mason Island carrying away the provisions of twenty-six families. The account stated that beds and dressers were found miles away, smashed on the mainland shores.

It's a pity that I don't have the low tide today as I could have followed the shoreline on Mweenish on my return run. Instead, I double back on the country road. The cows are mooing like crazy now as I run past. In fact, all this weekend I'm hearing the loud sounds from cows, horses, donkeys, and birds. Obviously, the farm animals are not used to too many strangers around here. I finally make my way back over the two causeways to Carna, following a loop road that brings me to the village where I had parked my car.

Stage 76 Revisited: Saturday 9 March 2024 Finis (or Feenish) Island, Connemara, Co. Galway: 12.9 km or 8.0 miles.

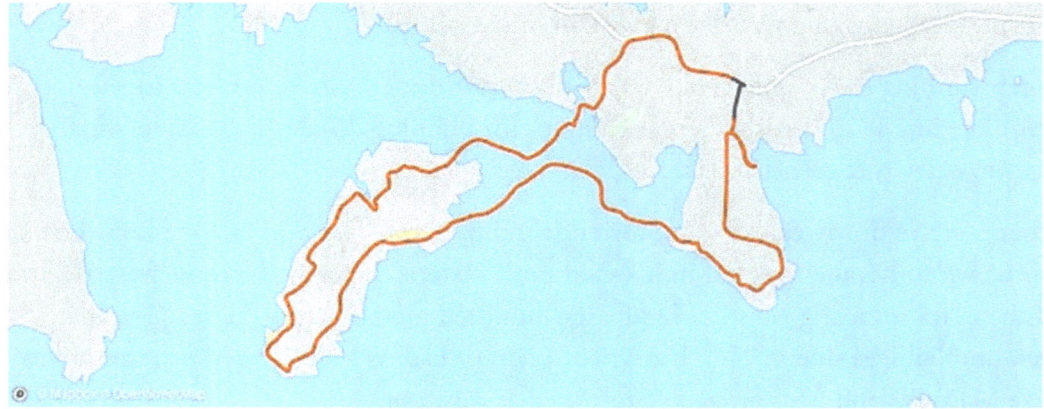

Finis Island: I was able to walk over through the sand from the east side.

CONNACHT COASTAL RUN

On my way out to Finis Island I decided to stop off at Oughterard and do the parkrun. Maybe this wasn't such a good idea, as I'll explain later, even if I did get the North Down AC tourism award. After parkrun I continued driving into Connemara, taking a left turn at Maam Cross. After passing Cill Chiarain I parked my car at a small crossroads at Tigh Leavy's Pub and headed towards the shore. I briefly ran down to Ardmore Quay but then backtracked a little, following the *Tra* sign and circled around the peninsula. Out in the sea I spotted two islands, Bior Mor and Bior Beag. Hard to believe seventeen people once lived there, according to the 1901 census. Eventually in the distance I spot it, Finis Island, in all its glory. It's low tide now and there's a huge stretch of open sand in front of me. I arrive on the island on the sandy east side.

So many lovely beaches on Finis Island

It's turning out to be a sunny day and all along this side of the island there are beautiful white beaches, one after the other. I continue south, circling the island but don't meet anyone at all during the morning. However, there is evidence of settlement on Finis Island over 4,000 years ago, long before Saint MacDara came to this area in the sixth century. In the 1901 Census there were 23 houses listed and all were occupied. As I run along the west side, I spot a few of these deserted houses. They might be old buildings but still look quite sturdy and well built. I see only one modern house which is probably used as a holiday home.

Deserted houses: Nobody lives on Finis Island anymore

When I eventually come back to the north of the island, I was surprised that the tide had come in so quickly. I can't see any obvious causeway and start to worry. There's an expanse of water between me and the mainland. Earlier I had checked online with two different websites, but it turns out that their tide indications were ninety minutes different to the actual tide times. Lucky for me the water is still shallow enough for me to make my way across. By the time I reached the other side my legs and feet are freezing. However, I was so relieved to be back on the mainland and the best way to stay warm was to keep running. I soon found a country lane and felt like an escaped prisoner as I sprinted all the way back to the crossroads where I'd parked my car. I learned an important lesson today to always check with local knowledge as regards tide times.

STAGE 77

Co. Galway: Cill Chiarain to Rosmuc

Sunday 30 October 2022

14.6 km or 9.1 miles

'Sometimes my heart hath shaken with great joy to see a leaping squirrel in a tree, or some green hill where shadows drifted by'
(from The Wayfarer by Padraig Pearse)

I wake about 7.00am in the house we're staying in at Cill Chiarain. I have a vague plan today about how far I'll get but first I'm waiting for the heavy rain to stop. This section is hillier than I expected, especially with the granite hills of Cnoc Mordain (Knockmorden) on my left side as I run (and sometimes walk) along the road.

I decide not to gamble any more with my good fortune of avoiding the rain this weekend and so, I decide to finish today's stage at Padraig Pearse's Cottage in Rosmuc. Also, I'm conscious that this would be an easy place for Maureen and Brian to meet me later and a well-known location to begin the next stage of the Coastal Run (probably on 11 February 2023 which will be the sixth anniversary of the start of my coastal adventure).

I've been to Pearse's Cottage a few times before. I was here with my children twice in the last twenty years and I first visited the cottage over fifty years ago with my own parents. I'm also old enough to remember the fiftieth anniversary of the 1916 Rising and I can recall learning the Irish Proclamation off-by-heart in St Patrick's Primary School in Galway City. Of course, it was Padraig Pearse who most likely composed the Proclamation.

Pearse famously recited it out outside the GPO in Dublin on Easter Monday 1916 to an ***'amused and bemused audience'.***

Padraig Pearse's Cottage, Rosmuc.

The Cottage itself is situated on an elevated site by Loch Oiriulach and was a summer retreat for Pearse between 1903 and 1915. He was inspired to write at the cottage, and it is accepted that he composed another famous and powerful speech here in July 1915. This was the graveside oration that Pearse gave for O'Donovan Rossa in Dublin on 1 August 1915,

Today, beside the Cottage, there is large Cultural Centre just off the A340 at Rosmuc (Ionad Culturtha an Phiarsaigh). While waiting for Maureen and Brian to arrive I was able to enjoy the exhibition. I might not have been a great admirer of Pearse and the men of Dublin 1916, but I do recognise that they were indeed brave men. To me the real heroes of Irish Nationalism were Parnell and Davitt who campaigned for land rights especially in the west of Ireland. In fact, on the very day of the Easter Rising on Monday 24th April 1916, my own grandfather was among a group of farmers in East Galway who were protesting about land ownership.

Pearse getting ready to speak at O'Donovan Rossa's funeral: 1st August 1915

So, while Pearse was reading out the Proclamation outside the GPO, my grandfather was among a team of men *'driving cattle'* to a landlord's home. Driving Cattle was a protest method used to highlight land ownership. My grandfather and three of his neighbours spent nine weeks in jail before they were released. However, Padraig Pearse only had nine days in prison and then he was executed (without any trial) on the 3rd of may 1916. Even I was shocked (after researching) that the executions of the 1916 leaders took place so quickly after Easter Monday (24th April)

While I was at the Visitor Centre in Connemara (just beside Pearse's Cottage) I was also able to hear Padraig Pearse's famous speech that he gave at O'Donovan Rossa's funeral in August 1915.

In his speech Pearse criticises the British Establishment or the 'Defenders of the Realm' as he calls them. His words are full of emotion, and he keeps building up momentum to the conclusion of his famous oration.

'The Defenders of this Realm think that they have pacified Ireland. They think that they have foreseen everything, think that they have provided against everything; but the fools, the fools, the fools – they have left us our Fenian dead; and while Ireland holds these graves, Ireland unfree shall never be at peace.'

It's well known that the men who occupied the GPO and other government buildings during Easter 1916 might have been easily forgotten about. Most Dubliners at the time were not impressed by the Irish rebels and when they were arrested, they got little sympathy from the locals. However, after the swift executions of the men (and without any trial), public opinion began to change. Ironically Pearse's words at O'Donovan Rossa's funeral came back to haunt the British establishment *'the fools, they have left us our fenian dead'*. As time passed the dead leaders of 1916 became heroes and martyrs.

STAGE 78

❖

Co. Galway: Rosmuc Peninsula:

Saturday 11 February 2023

35.2 km or 21.9 miles

'I used to hope that my physical experience of Connemara would burn through all these layers of tracing paper into the final drawing, making it not just a factual record, but an expression of a feeling.'
(Tim Robinson talking about making his own map)

I'm back in the Galway Gaeltacht after having a winter break. Rosmuc might not have the most beautiful sounding name. It means *'peninsula of rounded hills'*. The 'muc' is a more direct Irish translation for pig which has the same shape as rounded hills. However, Rosmuc has inspired five men who have all played a big part in the history of our country. I refer later to these characters; I call them the four horsemen (and one donkey man!) of Rosmuc. We should remember too, that between 1895 and 1935 the Galway to Clifden railway was operating and this made Connemara more accessible for visitors. The train stopped in Maam Cross which is only 13km from Rosmuc. Originally when the rail route to Clifden was discussed, locals in Connemara would have preferred it if the line took a coastal route through Carraroe. Also, this alternative course would have included a stop in Screeb, which is only 4km from Pearse's cottage.

I talked in the last few stages about myself and how I recently got my bloods checked. I had discovered that my iron levels were very low. I needed to take a dose of tablets for a few weeks and eat more foods with iron (like eggs, kale, and spinach). Now at last I am beginning to see the benefit of this diet. Crawfordsburn parkrun in North Down is one of the toughest parkruns in the country, but I struggled more than usual with my times during 2022, not been able to get under 25 minutes all year. Since November though I have gradually improved my time and last week I recorded 22.08 minutes for the 5k at Crawfordsburn.

I begin today's run at Pearse's Visitor Centre, take a right turn on the R340 and then after about 500 metres run down into the townland of Rosmuc itself. After about 2km I take a left at Tamhna Bhig to the pier at *'Snamh na Bo'* (swimming place of cows). At low tide, cattle would be encouraged to swim across the bay to the Camus peninsula, crossing through the small island of Dunmanus. In the 1800's there was a plan to build a road or bridge across here and even today there are obvious signs of a wide causeway on Dunmanus which was never completed.

I follow the road to the SE corner of the peninsula to Silear Pier. In the late 17th century, it was discovered that soda and potash, important chemicals in the soap and glass industries, could be extracted from burning seaweed. After being cut, the seaweed was brought up from the shoreline, dried and kept in a cellar (silear). Seaweed also has a natural source of vitamins for our bodies and benefits our bone health.

After leaving the Silear pier I joined the South Shore Road (Bothar Cheaimil). In his excellent book *A little Gaelic Kingdom'*, Tim Robinson explains how a section of this shore road is called *'Straidhp an Tae'* (tea strip) because there was so much tea drinking when people were cutting turf in the bog. I should point out that later in the week, on Leitir Moir island, I passed a harbour called An Sruthan Bui (the yellow stream) and I couldn't help wondering were these two place names connected! We all know what happens when you drink too much tea!

I take a left turn at the end of the Shore Road and head down to the SW corner of the peninsula. On the way there I took a brief detour down to the shore to Gairfean. There was a shop here, even up to the 1980's owned by Padraic O'Conaire's family (I'll talk about him later). Today this seems such a remote place to have a convenient store, right at the very bottom of the Rosmuc peninsula. However, looking at the map, Beal an Daingin is across the bay to the east and all the islands around Leitir Moir are close by to the south. Cill Chiarain and Carna are not too far away to the west. Traveling by sea, Gairfean is right in the middle of south Connemara!

I reach the SW corner of the Rosmuc Peninsula. Tim Robinson walked along this coastline in 1980 and really did stick to the coast. He was so thorough in finding exact meanings for areas and refers here to a wee rock lagoon called ***'Lochan an Phriosuin'*** (the pool of the prison), so called because a fisherman could get trapped by the tide in their boat if they rowed in at high tide and left it too late to leave the lagoon.

I backtrack and head towards the two islands on the west side of the peninsula. I really feel I'm in the Gaeltacht now. Everyone I hear is speaking Irish and I try to use the few words I know. I pass a man on the way and ask him ***'an bhfuil an taoide amach'*** (is the tide out). He replies in Irish ***'ta'*** and when I reach a pier, I start to run across to Oilean Mor. As I'm arriving on the island there is an old man coming towards me. I think he's the only inhabitant and he's taking advantage of the low tide to do his shopping on the mainland.

There is a path that runs right through Oilean Mor for about 1km. It starts as a rocky trail but progresses into a beautiful grassy boreen and then ends up as a muddy path as I get closer to an tOilean Iarthach (Western Isle). Even at low tide, crossing over to this second island is treacherous. Steppingstones are covered in wet seaweed, and I debated with myself whether I should attempt to go over. I'm glad I made the extra effort as I was thinking I'll probably never be back here again. It's hard to believe that there was once a school on this western island. It later moved to Oilean Mor which was closer to the mainland.

I leave the two islands and after about 500 metres I take a rough trail which leads me to Sean Bhaile (old town). In front of me, and down a hill, I see a quaint little pier with the Twelve Pins spread across in the near distance. I know immediately that this is the place described so eloquently by Tim Robinson ***'a little harbour whence one might imagine souls setting forth into an eternity of ever-changing waters and mountains'***

'Harbour of Souls' at Cill Bhreacain, Rosmuc Peninsula

I leave the *'harbour of souls'* and run north along the main Rosmuc road, taking a left turn after the cemetery. I join the R340 about 2km west of Pearse's Cottage and this allows me to loop around from the west side, back to my starting point at the Visitor Centre.

On my car journey back to Galway, I enjoy listening to the Ireland v France rugby international. It turns out to be an epic match. Just as I'm arriving in the city, the excited radio commentator loses his voice completely when Gary Ringrose goes over for a match-winning try for Ireland. So, a very satisfying day all round.

The four horsemen (and one donkeyman!) of Rosmuc

I mentioned some of these people already in my Rosmuc adventure. All had ties to this area, and all played some part in the history and development of Ireland.

Padraic O'Conaire: (1882-1928): I'll start with the donkey man. Padraic was born in the southern tip of the peninsula, in Gairfean (where his family had the shop). He described journeys around Rosmuc on his donkey in his most famous book, *'Mo Asal Beag Dubh'*. Anyone who grew up in Galway City (like I did) would be very familiar with O'Conaire's sitting statue in Eyre Square which had been there since 1935. His statue was very popular until it was decapitated by four men in 1999. It was repaired (head put back on) at a cost of £50,000.

Padraig Pearse: (1879-1916): I referred to him in more detail previously (see Stage 77). He wrote short stories and poems and gave that famous speech at O'Donovan Rossa's funeral in August 1915 which elevated him to the leader of the 1916 rebellion. As I said last time, I can imagine him wandering the boreens in Rosmuc, practicing and reciting those famous words. In fact, we know that Pearse did walk all round the peninsula as one of his tales was called *'Na Boithre'*. Boithre translates as roads, lanes or boreens and in his story Pearse covers every townland on the Rosmuc peninsula. Interestingly Bothar comes from the Irish word *'Bo'* which means cow. The first roads were really just cow trails.

Alexander Nimmo: (1783-1832): I came across his name so many times on my coastal run as he built most of the piers and harbours in Ireland. He also took a shine to Connemara and especially the Rosmuc area and helped open it up to travellers and traders. By developing roads and bridges *'he made its crooked ways straight.'* Even up to the 19th century there were no proper roads in Connemara, and they often took a longer route to avoid hills, rivers, and streams.

Sean Mannion: (born 1956) Sean is a famous boxer who is always very proud of his Rosmuc roots. His book was titled *'The man who was never knocked down'*. Not many fighters can say that. Mannion even got a shot at the vacant WBA title in 1984. His opponent at Madison Square Garden was Mike McCallum (who Ring Magazine ranked as the second greatest light middleweight boxer of all time). However, a month before the big fight, Mannion endured a severe cut to his right eye in training which greatly hindered his chance.

Tim Robinson: (1935-2020): Finally, I must talk about my own local hero, Tim Robinson. Tim really did stick to walking the coast, no matter how long it took, and created detailed maps of the area. Sadly, he died of Covid in March 2020. He was 85 years old but left a remarkable history of the Aran Islands, the Burren and Connemara. He called it *'the ABC of earth's wonders'*. Robinson maintained that every place name had a meaning, whether it was a story or something of historical local interest. He said that every corner of Connemara conveys a message like a boardgame.

I love to quote Tim Robinson's most famous phrase about him mapping the coast

'While walking the land, I am the pen on the paper; while drawing this map, my pen is myself, walking the land'.

It reminds me of what Van Gogh once said, *'I dream of painting, and I paint my dreams'*

Tim Robinson describes the pleasure of being out in the wilds of Connemara. *'I get such joy out of being out exploring this landscape and being alone in it, out in the bogs or up on the hills, or on the shore. I feel it's a terrible shame that very few people are enjoying that. I never, ever meet anybody.'*

I also identify with Tim's comments. I hardly meet anyone along the coast on my travels. I know it's only February but even on a Saturday in July it's rare to see anybody, especially if you go a mile or two off the beaten track.

STAGE 79

Co. Galway: Rosmuc to Beal an Daingin

Monday 13 February 2023

27.1 km or 16.8 miles

With my brother Anthony at Pearse's Cottage, Rosmuc

I have to thank my big brother Anthony (and Brian's Godfather, known as Uncle Tony) for helping me with the logistics today. We left Galway City in two cars at about 8.30am and headed for Beal an Daingin (today's finish line) where I left my own car. Anthony then drove me to Rosmuc to start my run.

There's a wee breeze from the south, but perfect running conditions with lovely sunshine all morning. I run pass Screeb House, a fishing lodge built in 1865 where Lord and Lady Dudley lived. Women also paid an important part in developing Connemara and Lady Dudley established a fund to help pay for district nurses in rural areas. The nurses travelled by bicycle along unpaved roads or walked across bogs and mountains to reach remote dwellings. They worked seven days a week and were always on call.

Just after Screeb, I take the main road south along the R336 and a right into Camas Uachtair. The translation of Camus is crooked, and it is indeed a crooked and windy road around this peninsula.

Camus residents are known by their nickname of Maicíní. At the top of Camus Hill is the big O sculpture which looks quite spectacular on a clear sunny morning like today. I notice some words on the big ring.

> *'The Twelve Pins came in sight and Pearse waved his hand here and there over the land, naming lake, mountain and district away to the Joyce Country under its purple mist.'*

The big O of Camus

This quotation is by Desmond Ryan who was a friend and great admirer of Padraig Pearse. Ryan himself was with Pearse in the GPO during the 1916 Rising and recalls hearing a volunteer shout to Post Office officials as they entered the GPO: *'This ain't no half-arsed revolution. This is the business'* Although that phrase sounds more like something that Newman or Redford might have said in Butch Cassidy and the Sundance Kid.

I return to the main road (R336) but again, I don't have to stay on it for long. After passing the school, and at a sign that says 'Madra', I take a right.

It's another crooked road along here that leads me to a small but modern bridge. This area is called *'Muiceanach idir Dhá Sháile'*, meaning 'pig-marsh between two sea inlets'. It was previously anglicised as one long word, *Muckanaghederdauhaulia* and once known as the longest named place in Ireland. However, it has now (thankfully) reverted back to its proper Irish name.

This example shows how stupid this whole translation business had been. It's a subject close to Tim Robinson's heart and he describes it well when he says, *'Irish place names dry out when anglicised, like twigs snapped off from a tree'.*

Once I cross the Cinn Mhara bridge I take a left and then I had to decide about whether I'd continue along the bog road south, or take a chance, by running along a rough boreen to the right which crosses over parts of Camus Bay and Loch an Aibhinn. I knew this second option was risky. I decided to go for it as I knew the tide was going out (and already about halfway there). The trail here was hit or miss, sometimes disappearing completely but at least the weather was dry and sunny. I crossed over two rocky causeways that were shaped like proper roads and were so wide that I've concluded there must have once been a pre-famine plan to build a proper bypass route from here across the sea to Beal an Daingin.

I kept going, knowing that I was going to have to cross a final sea-channel. The terrain was becoming rougher too and there was lots of heather, small trees, and thorny brambles. At first it looked as if the sea-crossing would be too wide (and deep), so I was resigned to going back all the way and taking the bog road south. However, through the brambles I spotted a narrower channel and made my way down through slippery rocks. I dipped my shoes in the water and made my way across. It was a short crossing, and the water hardly came up to my knees.

So pleased to reach this side of the sea inlet

Reaching the other side of the sea inlet, I only needed to climb up a grassy bank. I was very pleased with myself for finally reaching the west side of the channel. Afterwards I sat on a stone wall and rewarded myself with some chocolate. I had a real sense of achievement as I had looked at this crossing so many times on ordnance survey and on google maps.

Once on this side I could also see the ***'pre-famine road'*** that seemed to be heading down towards the sea. It was probably going to join up with a proposed bridge across the narrow sea (towards Camus). I can only conclude that this project, like many others, was started during the famine years and never finished because people were dying or leaving the area.

Just north of Beal an Daingin I took a turn down towards the coast. There I saw a new cemetery at the bottom of the hill and opposite it was, what looked like an older graveyard, on a small hill by the sea. I suspected that this was another Cillin (a resting-place for unbaptised children that weren't allowed to be buried in a proper cemetery). Sure enough, I learned later that this site was called *'Cnocan na Leanbh'* (the hillock of the infants)

Cnocan na Leanbh where unbaptised babies were buried

It was just about 2.00pm as I ran the last mile or two to the Costcutter shop in Beal an Daingin. Still dry, sunny, and now 12 degrees. Not bad for early February.

STAGE 80

❖

Co. Galway: Beal an Daingin loop, (circling islands of Eanach Mheain & Leitir Moir)

Thursday 16 February 2023

28.8 km or 17.9 miles

I drove out from Galway City this morning, parking my car again in front of the Costcutter in Beal an Daingin. I am heading into island country or *'Ceantar Na Oilean'* as this area is called. I cross the first causeway (Bealandangan Bridge) and then a second one, **Oilean na d'Trachta** which brings me onto Leitir Moir island itself.

I continue running for another 2km, through the island, as far as the church where I take a right turn on the southern shore. Along here I spotted a small memorial in front of a house with the initials FDNY. The inscription says, *'Teach an Fir Doiteain Sean'.* (House of the fireman, Sean) and had the 9/11 date on it too. I was reading about the 2001 disaster, and it is estimated that about 1,000 of those who died had Irish connections. Sadly, over 200 Claddagh Rings were reclaimed from Ground Zero.

This western part of Leitir Moir is called Leitir Calaidh and shortly, I take a left, signposted, *'An Ros and Inis Bearachain'.* Bearachain is an island about 500 metres off the coast and this is the best route to take to get there. Further west on Gorumna Island, Bearachain used to be accessible by foot but only at a very low tide, and by using a long series of causeways and steppingstones.

I follow the crooked road signposted to 'An Ros' and it brings me down to a pier. A dog is barking, watching my every move and a quartet of donkeys stare at me as I run pass. I don't see any humans at all, which is no surprise on this coastal adventure of mine.

I continue north as my plan is to circle Leitir Moir. However, when the country road ends, I must rough it across the bog. A pathetic sign, that has seen better days, shows an arrow pointing upwards and a faded picture of a walker. Welcome once again to the Irish coastal path which, by the way, doesn't exist! At least there are rocks to clamber over, which is slightly better than boggy fields. However, suddenly the rain comes down, so I need to be extra careful on the slippery stones.

I spot a lone cow (or bull) in front of me. Ever since my experience in Donegal (when I was chased by a herd of cattle), cows have become my least favourite animal. Furthermore, I have just been reading about an episode that happened not far from here, about 4km from Maam Cross. The area I'm referring to is called *'Doirin na gCos Fuar'* (small wood of the cold feet). A farmer was killed by a bull in a wood and then eaten by the animal. All they found of the dead man was his boots with the feet still in them!

Soon I come to a harbour, but after that I somehow miss the coastal road on my left. Instead, I follow a road south through the island. I actually made more work for myself coming this way. I didn't realise my mistake until I arrived back at Leitir Moir Church.

So, I head north again, crossing na d'Trachte causeway but this time taking a left onto Eanach Mheain island. I'm feeling pretty miserable now with the rain coming down and hungry too.

It actually turned out to be quite a pleasant experience running around Eanach Mheain. I take a left down to the pier on the west of the island but on my return journey I follow a trail that brings me onto *'Connemara Isles Golf Course'*. No surprise that there are no golfers here today. Part of the course is on another wee island Laidhean which is joined to Eanach Mheain by a short causeway. I'm able to circle this tiny island completely.

Guinness barrels have arrived! Ready for new golf season

I eventually follow the coast to the Golf Club House on the east side of Eanach Mheain. It's the only Thatched Club House in Ireland and the ancestral home of the Lynch family who founded the course in 1993. I head back towards my finish point at Beal an Daingin, as the rain comes down. Still, I feel a real sense of achievement having completed three runs (and 91km) in six days.

STAGE 81

Co. Galway: Gorumna Island, Connemara

Saturday 25 March 2023

32.8 km or 20.4 miles

'Is fada an bothar nach bhfuil casadh ann'
(the road is long, in which there is no turn)

I parked in the big car park just opposite the church in Leitir Moir. Two workmen are emptying the bins and chatting in Irish as I look across towards Gorumna island. Already here in *'Ceantar na nOilean'* (the islands district), it's a completely different world to Galway's busy city. My schedule today was to run around the islands of Gorumna and Leitir Meallain. However, as sometimes happens on this adventure of mine, things did not go according to plan. More about that later.

I decided to run clockwise today (sea on my left) to avail of the low tide later in the afternoon on the western side of Gorumna, which I wanted to coincide with me getting to *'Bothar na nOilean'*. First of all, I cross the long Charraig an Logain bridge and arrive on Gorumna island. The causeway was built around 1898 and before that there was a footpath that could only be crossed at a very low tide.

After about 2km, I turn left at a small crossroads and shortly arrive at a coastal trail, *'Luibin Gharumna'* which eventually takes me to 'An Tra Bhain' (white beach). In olden times this was a gathering place for pilgrims to the Aran Islands. People from Gorumna

Island and Leitir Moir looked across to Aran (only 12km away) and saw it as a spiritual and holy place.

There was a tragedy here in the 1860's. Four brothers drowned when their currach was rammed by a bigger sailing boat. Their sister Brid Ni Mhaille composed a sad lament for her siblings. The song is called *'Amhran Na Tra Bhaine'* and it is still a popular song in Connemara. It was even recorded by Fiachna O'Braonain of the Hot House Flowers. Although Fiachna was born and reared in Dublin he has strong family connections with this part of Connemara and considers Irish his first language.

It is now a lovely sunny morning here in South Connemara. Out in the bay, I can see *'Oilean an Anama'* (island of the souls). This beautiful area and the spring-like weather is indeed good for the soul. I eventually arrive at a small harbour, and this is where things started to go wrong. In my defence, it's easy to get confused as there are so many quays and piers in this area. Of course, the only mode of transport here up to the late 19th century was by boat.

I was reading last week in the Irish Times *'Russian ships return to Ireland's west coast'*, They reported that two Russian ships *'The Umka'* and *'The Bakhtemir'* were spotted off the coast of Co. Galway this week. A few years ago, we might have laughed this off, but with the Russian invasion of Ukraine, it's not such a joke anymore. The two ships were heading south and had left the Irish Exclusive Zone but then they turned around again and sailed up the west coast. Sometimes I feel I'm the only person out here in this corner of Connemara and I'm not sure what I would do if I spotted a Russian ship coming ashore.

Anyway, I leave the harbour and follow the road inland. I thought I was running south of Loch Bhaile, but I was actually running along Loch Hoirbeaird. To compound my mistake, I ended up taking a right turn (instead of a left) at a T junction.

Sir Roger Casement agus Na hOileain

In the early 1900's Casement started a relief fund when he heard of people in this area dying of typhus. He was executed as an Irish rebel in 1916 but had previously earned his British Knighthood by standing up for those suffering abuse in the Belgium Congo. Casement also always highlighted the oppressed in Connemara and knew the lessons from the famine were not really learnt by the British. He maintained that *'only Irishmen and Irish women could clean up filthy corners of the so-called United Kingdom'*

William Cadbury also made generous contributions to Casement's Relief fund and later Cadbury set up his own charitable trust in 1919. Talking of Cadbury reminds me to have my own chocolate break! (Although it is still lent and I'm off sweets, I've given myself an exemption today!)

I continue along the main Gorumna road heading west and eventually I come to a short causeway, ***Drochead Chaigheil,*** that finally takes me to the island of Leitir Meallain.

Crossing over to Leitir Meallain

I had originally planned to circle Leitir Meallain today but after taking a couple of wrong turns earlier, I decide to postpone exploring this island until my next trip to Co. Galway.

However, I do run as far as the crossroads on the island and visit the Heritage Centre there.

I decide to reward (and console) myself at the Heritage Centre with tea and a delicious fruit scone. I struggle with my Irish when I'm ordering but I'm determined not to speak any English as I'm in the heart of the Gaeltacht now. I sit outside and enjoy the beautiful sunshine. Sometimes you just have to enjoy the moment and I did so as I tucked into my late morning snack.

I retrace my steps, leave Leitir Meallain and head back across the short bridge to Gorumna Island. As I'm crossing the causeway I pause as I meet a funeral hearse followed by lots of cars. The deceased is being taken for burial to Reilig Chugeal cemetery on the Leitir Meallain side of the causeway. I stop running and cross myself. Something I hadn't done for a while, but it seemed the proper thing to do in this situation. Then at a small crossroads at Baile na Cille, I take a left and pass through a hilly area aptly called *'An Cnoc'*. After a few miles a dog comes running towards me. The lady of the house quietens her animal, Sailor I think she called him. I take the opportunity to ask her about Inis Bearachain and *'Bothar na nOilean'* and she pointed me in the right direction.

Inis Bearachain

One of the first essays that the historian, Tim Robinson wrote was called *'Walking out to Islands'* in which he describes this hazardous route to Inis Bearachain island. *'Bothar na nOilean'* (road to the island) is marked on the OS map and is a series of causeways, rocks and stepping-stones totalling a mile long that will take you all the way to Inis Bearachain. Tim Robinson describes waiting here patiently for the tide to go out.

> *'Watching waters pour out like an unhurried river, until by degrees the first of the stepping stones loomed up to the slowly sinking surface'*

As it was already low tide when I arrived here, I didn't have to wait for the steppingstones to appear. I had no intention to walk the whole way to Inis Bearachain, but I wanted to test 'bothar na nOilean'. I struggled to cross over the first broken and rocky causeway that was covered in slippery seaweed. What a dangerous journey this must have been for the islanders. It would have been a long mile across these greasy rocks, especially as it was a battle against the tide and other elements. Still, it was interesting to experience some of the hardship my ancestors had to go through. The other interesting fact about Inis

Bearachain is that in 1935, families who lived on the island (and in other nearby islands) were relocated to Rathcairn in Co. Meath. Each Connemara family was given a Land Commission house, a small farm of about 20 acres, a sow, piglets, and basic equipment. In 1935 this move was also seen as a cultural benefit to the new Ireland; a plan to save the Irish language and to spread the Irish culture on the eastern side of the country.

Maybe someday I'll get to Inis Bearachain. From this side of Gorumna it looked like there are some beautiful sandy beaches and I bet the islanders who left this area, still pined for their beautiful ancestral home.

I continue along this coast road. The sun is shining now and it's a perfect day for running, although I am tired now. I stop at a pier at Glenn Trasna (crossing of the glen) and finish my second gel and some more Cadbury's chocolate. Eventually I come to a crossroads and take a left, passing the impressive GAA grounds at Naomh Anna. I make my way back over Charraig an Logain bridge to the island of Leitir Moir where I'd parked my car many hours earlier.

Stage 81 Revisited: Ballynakill Church, South Gorumna, Connemara: Sunday 7 May 2023: 3.8 km or 2.4 miles

I missed this area back in March when I took a wrong turn, so it made sense to return today as I was nearby, in Lettermullan. This graveyard has a combination of old handmade graves and modern headstones with the ancient church itself right in the middle of everything.

To reach this holy and special place you take a turn south at a small crossroads, signposted Reilig. The junction is about half a mile east of Leitir Meallain island. After walking through the graveyard and reading various headstones I found a narrow grassy path on the edge of the cemetery. I ran along this trail heading south all the way to the shore.

Grassy path from Ballynakill Church to the sea

Once I reached the sea, it was just a matter of following the coast eastwards until eventually I came to a pier, *'Ceibh Pholl ui Mhuirun'*. From the harbour, I followed the road north until I reached 'Lough Bhaile na Cille' and back to the graveyard where I started. Happy to have fully completed Stage 81 in case 'The Coastal Audit Committee' check up on me!

STAGE 82

Co. Galway: Leitir Meallain Island

Sunday 7 May 2023

14.1 km or 8.8 miles

'Don't abandon the main road for the sake of a shortcut' (Irish proverb)

Tim Robinson described this part of Connemara as *'a land without short cuts'* and in my experience, it is never worth taking any short cuts. You might miss something special!

At the main crossroads on the island, I head south which eventually leads down to the shore. I then cross over a rocky shoreline to reach a boreen that takes me all the way to the SW corner of Leitir Meallain. Across the sea, I can see Golam Island and its tall Signal Tower.

View towards Golam Head & Golam Island

There is also a clear view of the Aran Islands from here. The western isles are only about 12km across the sea but unfortunately there is no causeway to those islands. It is said that Ireland's third saint, Colmcille visited Golam Island, and this then became part of a pilgrimage route to the Aran Islands.

I thought I might be able to loop around the western end of Leitir Meallain but there is a 'no entry' sign on a farmer gate. Anyway, there are cows and a young calf in the field, so I'm pleased to run back the way I came.

Back at the crossroads I head north and after about 1km I take a left onto *'An Crapach'* (Crappagh Island). I venture slowly across the causeway, but I don't delay long on the island. I had read on-line about the farmer, Val Folan who runs an organic farm on An Crapach. I like the way he called this whole area an *'archipelago of islands'* - a perfect word and I think I'll steal it from him!

Causeway to Oilean na Crapach, Leitir Meallain

I also heard that the McDonagh Clan once owned Crapach Island and a branch of the family later moved to Galway City to set up Thomas McDonagh & Sons. Also, the parents of Oscar-nominated film director, Martin McDonagh come from this area.

Further west I can see the islands of Fraochoilean Beag and Fraochoilean Mor but there are no causeways to these islands.

From 'An Crapach' I retrace my steps and head further north and cross a short causeway to Foirnis (Furnace) island. I have just realised to reach Foirnis from Beal an Daingin you need to cross five causeways! The road goes to the very top of this island and then there is a grassy path that takes me onto a beach with very soft sand. I am now very close to Daighinis (Dinish) Island. Even at low tide, I don't think you could walk across. However, it does look extremely attractive with a lovely sandy beach visible across the narrow channel.

The Ferryman of Dinish Island

In 1905, John Millington Synge and Jack B Yeats toured this area as part of an assignment for the Guardian Newspaper, who were supporting relief in the west of Ireland. Synge drafted an essay about a boatman he met, 'the Ferryman of Dinish', who did not seem happy with his life.

> *"I don't know what way I'm to go on living in this place that the Lord created last."*

I remember when I was in north Mayo on a beautiful July morning I heard a similar phrase from an old man, but he spoke it with joy and pride. He described his home on the Mullet peninsula as *'The last place God made'*.

Gap between Islands of Foirnis and Dinish, Leitir Meallain

Unfortunately, for me, there was no ferryman or woman to take me across to Dinish Island, so I had to retrace my steps and head south again.

On the way back I did take a right turn down to a pier *'Ceibh nua Fhoirnise'* which is quite close to Inis Eirc Island (Inisherk). Nobody has lived on this island since 1960 but some houses are still quite visible across the sea. I leave the pier and run south all the way back to my car at the crossroads. It is still only 9.45am and I'm delighted to have completed the island of Lettermullan. That means I have now done the whole *'archipelago of islands'* or as it's locally called, *'Ceantar na nOilean'*.

STAGE 83

Co. Galway: Beal an Daingin to Casla

Saturday 6 May 2023

39.1 km or 24.3 miles

'It is ok to feel whatever you're feeling and to know that it's temporary' Danny Quigley reflection on depression and suicidal thoughts

Cheathru Rua translates as the *'reddish quarter'* referring more to the brown boggy terrain. Not that I noticed much about the colour of the area when I arrived in pitch dark at 4.00am this morning. The reason for my early start was to tie into a *'Darkness into Light'* annual walk. These walks are organised by Pieta House in Dublin who provide counselling to anyone struggling with suicide or anybody impacted by suicide. There are hundreds of these annual events all over Ireland and they all began at 4.15am today, 6 May. I was privileged to be able to join the Carraroe Walk.

Darkness into Light Walk: Sometimes HOPE (Dochas) is all we need

It was so inspiring to see hundreds of people in this corner of Connemara supporting such a worthy cause. Before we started our walk, a lady gave a short talk, completely in Irish and finishing with *'An bhfuil sibh reidh?* Yes, we were all ready to go! On the walk I got chatting to Grainne and Jack Lynch who had come from Moycullen. Afterwards I joined them in the school hall for tea and biscuits.

As dawn was breaking, I began my run, heading north on the main R343 road. Just before I got to Casla (or Costelloe) I took a left turn, onto the R374 towards Beal an Daingin passing the Radio na Gaeltachta building.

Radio na Gaeltachta

In 1972, the Irish language radio station started broadcasting and in 1996, the TV Station, TG4 followed. Last year I saw a beautiful program to celebrate the fiftieth anniversary of 'Radio na Gaeltachta'. I was struck especially by this haunting song, *'Amhran na nGael'*, written and sung by the talented west Kerry musician, Meabh Ni Bheaglaoich. *'Cá bhfuil croí, anam, corp is spiorad na nGael'* (Where is the heart, soul, body, and spirit of the Gaels).

I continue along the R374 road towards Beal an Daingin, but I take a left turn back down into the Carraroe peninsula again. After another 3km I head west to Oilean na Rossa. It is just 7.00am and turning out to be a beautiful day as I cross the bridge over to the island. Such a quiet and peaceful place. I leave Rosroe Island and head south towards 'downtown Carraroe' keeping Loch an Mhuillin on my left. Passing this lake reminds me of a famous painting by the artist, Charles Lamb.

Charles Lamb and Eamon de Buitlear

Charles Lamb was an Ulster man who was encouraged to come and paint in Connemara by Padraig O'Conaire. Lamb then toured the area on horseback and settled in Carraroe. One of Lamb's famous paintings depicts a local woman washing clothes in Loch an Mhuillin. The sky is stormy and the reflection in the water of the cottage is broken up by the woman's washing.

Charles Lamb's painting at Loch an Mhuillin

The wildlife film maker, Eamon de Buitlear was Lamb's son-in-law and a regular visitor to Carraroe. Years ago, I remember watching his regular TV program, *'Amuigh Faoin Speir'*. Eamon was ahead of his time as regards highlighting nature and environmental issues.

I took a loop, via the coast, just before the main crossroads in the village which brought me eventually around to the beautiful waters of *'Loch na Caisleach'*

I sat on a wall here and enjoyed the view over Loch na Caisleach

I recently watched a beautiful Irish language (and Oscar nominated) film *'An Cailin Ciuin'*. Forty-six years ago, the first ever film, entirely in the Irish language, was called *'Poitin'*. This part of Connemara always had a tradition of poitin making going back as far as the 1600's. It was cheap and an easy drink to make – all you needed was yeast, sugar and of course potatoes! Until 1997 it was illegal to produce. Today's legal version is smoother with 'only' 40% alcohol. Originally, poitin was one of the strongest beverages in the world with alcohol content of up to 90%. In the olden days, many wee bottles of the beverage were smuggled to America and England, labelled *'Holy Water from Knock'*.

I took the road down to Caladh Thaidhg (named after Taidhg O' Cathain who owned boats in this area). When I reached Taidhg's pier I roughed it along the coast as far as *'Tra an Doilin'* where I meet two swimmers. I could see why they come here every day to this beautiful, secluded beach with its clear blue water. The beach is also called An Tra Choirealadh or the Coral Strand, because of its shiny coral shingles and sand.

At this stage I realised that it would be too difficult to stay strictly by the shore, so I took a road inland, Bothar Bui to the very bottom of the peninsula, Cora na Ronna. I was pleasantly surprised to find a coastal path along the southern shore. I figured it must have been an ancient trail from pre-famine days when there were thousands of people living in this area.

The wild flowers of Carraroe

I follow a boreen, Bothar an Chillin north and take a turn down towards the shore. I end up trampling through fields but then I have a moment of celebration when I see in the distance a graveyard. I know this is *'Tra na Reilige'* (cemetery strand). Nearby is an ancient medieval chapel, ***Tempeall MacAdhaigh,*** which was constructed by Saint Smocan. He came over from the Aran Islands and apparently built the church in just one day! Maybe he also got up early like I did this morning.

Tempeall MacAdhaigh, Carraroe - built in one day by Saint Smocan

Battle of Carraroe (Cath an Cheathru Rua)

I cannot leave Carraroe without referring to its most historical event. This happened in January 1880, and it refers to a dispute over evictions and land rights. There were several years of bad harvests. Tenants could not pay their rents and so notices of evictions were pinned to doors. People from around the county rallied to join the Carraroe people, including twelve boats from nearby villages and the Aran Islands. With just sticks and stones, the tenants and their allies defeated a large force of RIC men armed with rifles and bayonets.

This was the first successful attempt to prevent an eviction. The *'Land League'* had only been founded a couple of months previously by Charles Stewart Parnell and Michael Davitt. Davitt wrote that the landlords were *'a brood of cormorant vampires that has sucked the life blood out of the country'*. All these protests achieved a remarkable degree of success in the west of Ireland. Parnell and Davitt often referred to the 'Battle of Carraroe' in their American campaigns.

Oasis of greenery at Gleann Mor, Carraroe

Anyway, back to today. I leave the harbour and head inland but take a right turn along **'An Glenn Mor'**. Unlike the rest of Carraroe (or anywhere else in south Connemara) this area is a strange oasis of greenery with its trees, bushes, and lush pastures. It has also got the highest point in the peninsula, Barr an Doire (88 metres), which still isn't much of a hill.

At the harbour at Sruthan I take a left turn back down to the main village. The Eurospar where I left my car is now a hive of activity with a late morning buzz of shoppers. I sit on the boot of my car, enjoying some fresh Coffee and a warm scone - feeling very satisfied with myself.

STAGE 84

❖

Co. Galway: Casla (Costello) to An Spideal

Saturday 27 May 2023

33.6 km or 20.9 miles

'Shall I compare thee to a summer's day? Thou art more lovely and more temperate. Rough winds do shake the darling buds of May'

This is the first time I've quoted Shakespeare on my blog. I love that phrase *'the darling buds of May'*. I was thinking of it as I ran along the beautiful Co. Galway coast with all those wild flowers blooming in the May sunshine. I'm sad to say that my long love affair with Connemara is coming to an end this weekend as I arrive in Galway City. On the other hand, I am excited to finally reach my native town.

I park my car at the petrol station in Casla (or Costello as it was previously called.) It's 8.00am and I run along the R336, the Furnace Road. At the small crossroads I take a right turn as far as the quays at Rossaveel.

Ros an Mhil (Rossaveel) literally means *'wood of the whale (or sea monster)'* so now I might have to contend with enormous sea creatures. In fact, as recent as May 2021, there was a huge jellyfish caught here in Rossaveel. It was so rare that we don't even have an English (or Irish) word for it, just a scientific name, ***Thalassobathia pelagica***. Perhaps I shouldn't run too close to the shore today!

The whole harbour has been redeveloped and the government have said that Rossaveel's proximity to offshore projects and a deep-sea berth would provide an opportunity to take advantage of the wind industry. They have invested 25 million euro in the project. The massive Wind Turbine dominates the skyline for miles around. Rossaveel is also the main port for connecting to the Aran Islands. Having said all that, it is still very quiet at this time of the morning.

I decide to stay by the coast and rough it through rocks and fields. It's not a pleasant experience as I trample through gorse and thorn bushes and climb over a few electric fences. I can see the Martello Tower in the distance but it's not that easy to get to. Finally, I do reach the tower. The writer, Tim Robinson describes it as ***'just standing there like a giant's chess piece ready to make it move.'***

There were similar structures built all around Ireland in the early 1800's. These type of towers were strategically placed to stop a French invasion by Napoleon's army. That doesn't surprise me as it was only a few years before in 1798 that General Humbert arrived in north Mayo. (as I referred to back in Stage 47). Humbert's small army caused a lot of damage and embarrassment for the British establishment in Connacht.

Leaving the tower, I continue south and rough it along the coast to the bottom of the Rossaveel Hill. There is even a stile to climb over which gives me some encouragement that there might be some kind of path ahead.

There is no path on the other side of the stile. I run to the bottom of the peninsula and start to look out for a trail that will take me north again. However, there are cows here that give me darting looks so I circle around the peninsula and eventually I do find a boreen.

The old Martello Tower (early 1800's) and new Wind Turbine (early 2000's)

The hated Blakes

Tim Robinson writes about how 'the Blakes emptied the townland of 'Toin an Chnoic'. It was all part of the Blakes tidying up or clearing plan so that they could build their fortress, Cashel House on the shore a few miles further east at Tully, near Connemara Airport.

Boreen north from Toin an Chnoic

I should admit to a family connection as my great, great, grandmother was Bridget Blake. I had always been quite proud of the fact that I was related to one of fourteen tribes of Galway. I even know all the tribes, off by heart, Athy, Blake, Bodkin etc. However, in this part of Co. Galway my ancestors were referred to as *'the hated Blakes'*. The writer, Tim Robinson explains this *further 'adding insult to injury, the Blakes supported the Irish Church Mission in its efforts to convert their tenants to Protestantism. Having got their sixpence for attending services, the tenants would go straight to the Catholic chapel for Mass and contribute a penny, thus making a profit of five pence'.*

I proceed on the trail, loop around a narrow channel, and follow a coastal road south. I spot a lady in her front garden and ask her for a drink. Her name is Brid, and she kindly gets me a big glass of water. We have a lovely chat in the morning sunshine as Georgie, her cat, hides in the long grass.

I follow a trail signposted *'Sli Connemara'*, heading further south all the way to the shore. I'm lucky I did get that glass of water because I stay by the shore for the rest of the day and don't pass any more houses.

Sli Connemara: I read that this trail is *'a 220km way-marked route that begins in Galway City and winds its way out to Connemara'*. This is encouraging but I take this statement with a pinch of salt. It then says under 'advisory' that the route is not maintained, and maps are now obsolete. I think it was just another project that was too ambitious for a small country like ours.

The darling buds of May light up Connemara

Dr. Noel Browne

Passing the graveyard, Reilig Mhairois, I'm able to stay by the coast and decide to keep south of the lake, Lough na Creibhinne (or Lough Nagravin). The cemetery and the lake remind me of Noel Browne who was Minister for Health in the 1950's. He lived and retired in this area. Dr. Browne was ahead of his time - too far ahead of his time for the Catholic Church and for some of the medical profession. As a young Health Minister he eradicated tuberculosis (TB) and tried to bring in a National Health Service to Ireland. Even when he retired here in south Connemara in the 1970's he helped the local community. He encouraged a neighbour to fish in Lough na Creibhinne, which under an old system of private ownership, was forbidden. Noel Brown was a true socialist and fought for the less privileged all through his life. Dr Browne's mother and sister had been buried in a pauper's grave, both lost to tuberculosis. Brown just wanted *'to have an ordinary stone off a wall'* as a burial marker.

Near Indreabhan I spot two planes heading out to the Aran Islands. I have just passed Connemara Airport. It would be a perfect day to spend on the islands.

I'm surprised how easy this part of the coastline is to manoeuvre. However, after a while I found the rocky terrain, although flat, a bit sore on the feet. The hard surface would not be recommended if you were suffering from a dose of plantar fasciitis! However, a good pair of sturdy mountain boots would have made it a very pleasant walk. Still, there were also some grassy and trail sections along the way, which were perfect for the runner.

Graveyard for 'the unbaptised' with new memorial

I pass what was once a cemetery for the unbaptised, usually new-born babies. I've referred to these Cillineachs a few times in my blog and called it a kind of warped morality in not letting the unbaptised be buried in a proper graveyard. Today there is a monument on the shore trying to redress some of the past ideology.

And not far away, along the shore I come across another memorial. A World War 1 landmine exploded here on 15 June 1917. Hard to believe that any of the great wars came so close to Galway. When the landmine was first spotted on the beach, local people didn't understand what it was. Some men tried to tow it in to shore and when they realised that it might be dangerous, it was too late. It exploded, killing nine men. Afterwards, the British government insisted that *'none of their mines laid in or near Galway Bay'*. An inquest was held the very next day in Thigh Mhaimí Costello, now An Poitín Stil. Quickly a decision was reached and concluded that it was a German landmine. However, some argued that the prompt judgement taken, was to emphasise that there would be no compensation available from the then British government.

Memorial for nine men who lost lives in the 1917 Landmine

I continue following the coast. There are lots of small beaches along here. Even *'An Tra Mor'* isn't that big, despite its name.

The coastline gets uneven and rougher from now on. I cross another stream by way of a slippery causeway. However, I am getting close to my finish line. I know there is a bus at 13.41 from Spiddal to Casla (where I left my car). If I miss that, I will have to wait ninety minutes for the next one. I push on and when I finally reach the pier at Spiddal, I sprint up the hill and get to the town just before the bus arrives. When I get on the bus, I offer payment to the driver, but he says, ***'Were you the man I saw running at 8 o clock in Carna'.*** He nods me in for a free bus journey. It's a pleasant ending to a hard-working day.

STAGE 85

Co. Galway: An Spideal to Salthill

Sunday 28 May 2023:

20.8 km or 12.9 miles

I have a friend, Donald Smith (who also lives in Bangor, Co. Down) joining me today. It's the first time anyone has run with me since arriving in County Galway in Easter 2022. Donald, the flying Scotsman, had just completed a tough marathon in Co. Clare yesterday and so joined me for this stretch into Salthill. Even though I grew up in Galway city, I never realised, until now, that the name An Spideal derives from the word ospideal (hospital). Medical facilities were based in the area and there was a famine hospital here in the 1840's.

Near Furbo: Great to have Donald join me today

Donald and I start at the pier and loop around the coast to the main beach. We pass a statue here commemorating Martin O'Cadhain, the writer from Spiddal.

Martin O'Cadhain (1905-70) and the Irish Language

He dedicated his life to safeguarding the Irish language and maintained that *'Irish won't be saved without the Gaeltacht being saved'.* The number of Irish speakers decreased dramatically after the Great Famine of the 1840s when the language became associated with backwardness, poverty, and despair. There were still four million speakers of Irish on the eve of the famine in 1841, but by 1891 the figure had fallen to 680,000. Accelerating the decline was the fact that large numbers of Irish-speaking parents - believing that the language would hold back their children, who would mostly have to emigrate - stopped speaking to their children in Irish.

After leaving Spiddal, we realised that it would have been too hazardous to stay by the shore, so we run along the main road as far as Na Forbacha (Furbo) and then we rejoin the coast.

The terrain along here is tricky. Sometimes there is the odd trail but mostly it's an uneven, rocky section that's impossible to run on. We meet a few kids along here who are very curious about what we're doing. I tell them proudly that we're running around the coast of Ireland. One of them says *'but you're walking'*.

At Barna Harbour we're able to stay on the coast and rough it along the shore.

With 'Private Property' sign we had to make a detour inland sometimes

We arrive on Silverstrand or in Irish, *Tra na gCeann*, beach of the head/top. As a youngster in Galway city, I often cycled out here. It always felt a bit exotic, away from busy Salthill.

Running out to Gentian Hill, Salthill

It is a great pity that there is not some kind of coastal trail from Silver Strand to Salthill. It would be a beautiful walk from Blackrock to here.

So, Donald and I leave the beach, run up the hill and join the R336 towards Galway. Originally my plan was to finish today's run at Knocknacarra Community Centre, the home of Galway's parkrun. (this is where I'll start my next stage). However, I thought it would be easier today to tackle the headland, just south of Blackrock. I always believed this headland was called either Blakes Hill or Gentian Hill (after the wild blue flowers that grow there) but the name on the OS map is 'Oilean na Feamainne' (island of the seaweed).

So, we leave the Barna road just before the caravan parks, signposted Blakes Hill. At the end of a row of houses, we follow a grassy path that leads to a rocky shore under the corroding cliffs. We cross a narrow channel and eventually reach Oilean na Feamainne (or Gentian Hill). Donald and I climb up to the top of the headland and look for blue gentian flowers but couldn't find any. Still, it's such a beautiful quiet oasis, here so close to a busy city.

We slowly make our way back (more rocks) and reach the coastal pathway that takes us to Blackrock. After soaking our tired feet in the sea, Donald and I relax in the amphitheater opposite the diving boards. We sit alongside a few more spectators watching the brave swimmers jump into the sea and perform to the Galway public.

STAGE 86

Co. Galway: Knocknacarra to Oranmore

Saturday 8 July 2023

32.1 km or 19.9 miles

'We all returned back again and to Joyner's we did go. And we drank the health of man to man, for the clearing out of Grow'. A verse referring to my grandfather and neighbours who spent time in Galway Jail. More about this later.

As it's holiday time I was able to complete three different stages during the week. I am lucky to have such good company over this weekend as a few friends from NDAC (North Down Athletic Club) joined me. There were six runners who travelled down from Bangor to Galway last night. Helen, Neill, Alison, Steve, Sean, and Gerry (Helen & Sean are of course the original duo who completed all of Northern Ireland with me)

The week started badly. I wasn't feeling well on the previous Sunday and a test proved I had Covid. I was just about recovering for the trip to Galway when I heard the forecast for rain and strong winds. The plan was to start our adventure with the parkrun in Knocknacarra (hill of the city) and run into the town from there. However, on Friday night it was announced that that the Oranmore parkrun, on the east side of the city, was cancelled because of strong winds. I wasn't very hopeful for the Knocknacarra parkrun as the course takes you through Barna Woods. Eventually all seven of us turned up and despite the rain and wind, thankfully the parkrun did take place.

After our 5k run we head for Salthill and run to the diving boards at Blackrock. I was delighted that parents and children from Rosedale Special School were there to greet us. As you might know I've started supporting and raising funds for Rosedale over the last few months and it was so nice to chat to parents and their children at Blackrock.

After kicking the wall at the end of the prom (as all true Galwegians do!) the *'magnificent seven'* runners continue along the esplanade. With strong winds and some rain, it's not as busy as a normal Saturday in July. This whole area is very familiar to me. I lived in Rahoon Road until I was thirteen and Salthill was only about 2km away. The Irish name for Salthill is *'Bothar na Tra'* (the road to the beach).

The original Coastal Three on Salthill prom

We continue running along Grattan Road, which was once nick-named *'the ten-penny road'* as that was apparently the daily payrate workers received for building it in 1863. It was Miss Fanny Grattan who instigated the whole project. Her grandfather was Henry Grattan of *'Grattan's Parliament'* fame and the family-owned land in this area. Fanny suspended the rent to tenants and embarked on an ambitious project of building this relief road through her seaside property.

Back in 1863 a journalist in the local newspaper was impressed. *'The completion of the Grattan Road will add much to the beauty and salubrity of the handsomest of our sunburn districts'.*

On the city side of Grattan Road there is now a long slipway to Mutton Island which has a Lighthouse and sewage treatment plant. I think this has made Salthill a cleaner bathing area and even more salubrious! As the rain comes down, we run out to the island. It's worth the trip for the nice views on the way back, although a little hazy today. After returning we stay by the shoreline on the edge of the playing fields called 'South Park'. Growing up in Galway, we always referred to these fields as *'The Swamp'*. In fact, my first ever running experience was here. I was about ten years old and part of the school relay team. I remember training here in our bare feet.

At least the rain has stopped. After leaving 'The Swamp' we come to Nimmo's Pier. On my coastal run so far, I've come across so many harbours, bridges, and roads that the engineer Alexander Nimmo designed. However, this is the only pier in Ireland called after him.

At the Claddagh with Galway City behind

We are now in the Claddagh area. Originally this was a fishing village outside the walls of the city and always had its own traditions. Most people would have heard of the Claddagh Ring. The song, *'The old Claddagh Ring'* describes how it was handed down from mother to daughter and the words explain the ring's unique design.

> *'The crown and the crest to remind me of honour and clasping the heart that God's blessing would bring'.*

Back in the 1970's and long before the Claddagh Ring became fashionable, most young women in Galway had the ring. If a girl wore the ring with the heart facing out, it meant her heart was given away. No point in chatting her up! However, wearing the ring with the heart turned in, meant that a guy had a chance!

View from the Claddagh towards Long Walk

The sun is shining now as we cross over the river at Wolfe Tone Bridge, called after the famous leader of the 1798 rebellion. We take an immediate left after the bridge and run along a path by the Corrib that takes us through the heart of the city. I love this walk (or run) by the river. We first reach 'O'Brien's Bridge' which was the original crossing over the river.

The bridge separates the two schools I attended, St Patrick's Primary School (*'the Brothers'*) and St Joseph's Secondary (nicknamed *'The Bish'* because the Bishop of Galway once taught there).

St Patrick's is next to the ancient St Nicholas Church, which has huge town clocks that always told the correct time. Strangely though, the clocks are only on three sides of the church. There is no clock on the western facing end, just a blank circle. The story is that the despised Flaherty family lived in that direction and the establishment in the city (the fourteen tribes of Galway) would literally '*not even give them the time of the day*'.

Today, from the river, I can see my old classroom in St. Patrick's school. Every morning before classes began, we'd assemble in the schoolyard. The band would play some Irish tunes, and we would march around in formation. When the music had finished, a schoolboy would raise the Irish flag and we'd all sing the national anthem. I didn't realise it at the time, but locals and tourists would often come to watch our daily performance.

We continue running by the river and shortly we arrive at Galway's wonderful new bridge. It is just a footbridge, but I'm so impressed by it. Even though it is not physically on 'google maps', a name is mentioned *'Julia Morrissey Bridge'*. I know there is a campaign to have the bridge called after her, but I don't think it's official yet. Morrissey was a key figure in *'Cumann na mBan'* (the women's army). In 1916, she commanded a group of fifty women during Easter week, as part of the rebellion in Galway that was led by Liam Mellows. The two developed a close bond and ended up in a relationship, and it is said that Julia never recovered from Mellows' execution in 1922 (by his fellow Irishmen). In the 1930s, she ended up confined to the mental asylum in Ballinasloe. She didn't receive the state pension that had been set up for veteran republicans nor did she receive any medals recognising her contribution in 1916.

The bridge has now been official named as **'Droichead an Dóchais'** or the 'Bridge of Hope' and is dedicated **'to all those who have concerns about mental health'**. That is a good name too and everybody can identify with these sentiments.

The footbridge was only opened in May, and it leads to Galway's 'new' Cathedral which is almost sixty years old now. On this site, before the huge church was built, stood Galway Jail where my grandfather spent eleven weeks in prison.

Imprisonment of the Moylough Four

My father's father was one of the four men who served their time in Galway Gaol (now site of Galway Cathedral) in 1916. He was imprisoned for his part in the land protests in east Co. Galway. It was a peaceful objection where my grandfather and his neighbours drove cattle from farms owned by landlords back to the owner's house. One particular landlord, Mr. Fleming objected strongly to this kind of demonstration. My dad wrote about this in various articles for magazines and newspapers. He tells the story about his own father, as follows.

'Nineteen men from the area took part in the driving of cattle and sheep belonging to Mr. Fleming. (An area known as 'Grow'). When the party arrived at Fleming's with the stock, the latter was furious and threatened to shoot them. The men were eventually charged and appeared in Court in Dublin. Four of the men spent nine weeks in Galway Gaol and on their return from prison they were escorted to their homes by a group of musicians and were greeted by bonfires and banners'.

I'm one of the 'Galway Four' re-enacting 1916 land protesters and their arrest

I was privileged in April 2016 to be part of the hundred-year re-enactment of these land protests. Afterwards the four descendants of the prisoners had to speak. I said that 1916 was an important year and I compared the Cattle Driving protest in Galway with the other two historical events of 1916, the Battle of the Somme, and the Easter Rising in Dublin. I felt that that the Cattle Driving peaceful demonstrations were just as important. Nobody died in these land protests, and it was a successful campaign as my father concluded in his article.

'The story of the Moylough cattle driving in 1916, however, has an extremely happy ending, as before the termination of that decade, the lands in question were acquired by the Land Commission and practically every one of the families involved in the incidents referred to, benefited from the eventual land division'

Me again as part of 2016 re-enactment of 'cattle driving'

Back in 2023 we can continue along the river into the Woodquay and Waterside area. The old railway bridge to Clifden crossed the Corrib here and the huge bollards are clearly visible on the river. Trains only ran for forty years between 1895 and 1935 before they closed for economic reasons.

We try to follow the old railway line back to Galway's main railway station. This is an impossible task as the first part of the old railway line on the hill is completely overgrown and after that the line went underground. We run through an alleyway that brings us to a green area. I used to play Gaelic football here on what we called *'The Plots'*. We run up a steep hill called *'Hidden Valley'* (the others will thank me later for getting a wee hill in today's adventure!) We reach the Railway Station. I often think we are lucky in Galway as the train terminal is right in the middle of the city, just beside Eyre Square.

The green area in the Square is now officially called Kennedy Park after the US President who came to Galway in 1963, almost exactly sixty years ago. I'm just about old enough to remember having a wee American flag with all its colourful stars and stripes. Kennedy spoke in Eyre Square and made a comment about all the Galway people living in Boston and how the two cities are connected. ***'On a clear day you can see Boston'***, he said.

We're all feeling a bit thirsty (and hungry too) as the seven of us run through Kennedy Park and then head downtown through Galway's pedestrian area.

The two Wildes: On Shop Street at the start of the traffic free area there is a lovely sculpture on a bench showing Irish writer Oscar Wilde (1854-1900) and Estonian writer Eduard Vilde (1865-1933). They never actually met but they both shared a similar humour and wit.

I've often quoted Oscar Wilde on my coastal run with his apt phrase 'sand is for the feet of the runner'

Today Galway City is thronged with shoppers and tourists. We don't even attempt to run through the crowded streets, much easier to walk. In any case we decide to have a break. We order coffee and scones and sit outside in the sunshine on Mainguard Street.

With Leah Walsh (Davy's daughter) from Rosedale Special School

Davy Walsh, a parent from Rosedale stops to chat to us again. He introduces me to Joe Corcoran who played Gaelic Football years ago with my late brother Sean. They were both on the St. Michaels team that won the Co. Galway under-18 final in 1969. Furthermore, Joe had the honour of captaining the Galway Minor team that won the All-Ireland in 1970, beating a young Kerry team that were the backbone of their famous 1970's senior team.

With Joe Corcoran, captain of Galway's All-Ireland winning team

After our wee break, the seven of us continue running down High Street and Quay Street.

Spanish Parade & Spanish Arch

On Spanish Parade by the river, there is a small monument referring to Christopher Columbus which was gifted from his native city, Genoa in 1992. It says, *'on these shores he found sure signs of land beyond the Atlantic'*. Indeed in 1477 Columbus visited Galway and was convinced land lay to the west. He noted in one of his writings that *'many remarkable things have we seen, particularly in Galway where a man and woman of a most unusual aspect adrift in two boats'*.

As we are passing Columbus monument, there's a tour guide asking a young group why 1992 was so significant. I proudly raise my hand and answer that it was 500 years after Columbus discovered America. The tourists do not seem impressed with my expert knowledge!

At this stage, Alison, Steve, and Gerry leave us and head back to Salthill where their campervans are parked. Meanwhile, Helen, Neill, Sean, and I continue and run under the Spanish Arch.

We follow the shore on 'Long Walk' as per the opening line in Steve Earl's song, 'Galway Girl'.

'I took a stroll down the old Long Walk'

Maureen (Galway Girl) taking a stroll on the old Long Walk

We arrive at the Docks area and follow the road around towards Loch Atalia. We run under the bridge and then take an immediate left to the Galway Station to join *'the Line'* which is a path that runs along the railway track towards Renmore.

As we're running along the railway line, I can't help thinking about a young Swiss girl Manuela Riedo who was cruelly murdered here 2007. The murderer was found and convicted. The ***'Manuela Riedo Foundation'*** founded in her memory has raised one million euro. Funding has been used for counselling which provides support to victims and survivors of sexual assault and rape in Ireland.

When we reach Renmore, we run down to Ballyloughane beach. We then rough it a little along here as there is no proper path. We arrive at 'Waithman's Pier' called after the family that owned acres of land in this area. Most of it was compulsory purchased in 1940's to build a sanitorium (now Merlin Park hospital) for those suffering from tuberculosis.

It's too rocky to stay on the shore so we follow a trail that leads inland and crosses the gated railway line. The Blake family had their residence here at the railway crossing and used their power and influence. They were able to stop the train by tying a red flag to the gate. It meant that they didn't have the inconvenience of having to go all the way into the city to catch the train to Dublin!

We continue to Oranmore village and then via the Maree road (L4101). About 2km later we take a right turn along a narrow and windy road that eventually leads to Renville Park which is the home of Oranmore's parkrun.

We get a lovely surprise at our finish line when a few more Rosedale parents and their children meet us here. As a thank you, they also present me with a beautiful album with lovely pictures. It really made my day. I'm privileged to be able to help Rosedale Special School by raising funds through my coastal running.

And in Supermacs I meet my nephew Kevin and my great nieces

Stage 86 Revisited: Monday 11 March 2024: Hare Island, Renmore, Galway City: 4.7 km or 2.9 miles.

Although there is a causeway to this island it is only passable at a very low tide. In fact, today was the lowest tide of 2024 so I knew it was very safe to cross. It's exactly one kilometre along the causeway to reach the island but only about 700 metres to circle it completely.

There is a large lake or lagoon in the middle which probably accounts for half of the area of the whole island. From the top of a grassy hill, I had the perfect view of Galway Bay and I felt quite close to Mutton Island and Salthill. It's a beautiful spring morning, no wind or rain and almost feeling warm even though I'm standing in the middle of Galway Bay. If you are on Ballyloughane Beach at high tide, it's hard to imagine that you could ever walk to this island.

I first heard about Hare Island after reading Walter Macken's *'Rain on the Wind'* in which the main teenage characters do get stuck on the island overnight and must wait for the low tide in the morning. It's the quintessential Galway novel and one of my favourite books.

STAGE 87

Co. Galway: Renville, Oranmore to Clarinbridge

Sunday 9 July 2023

28.0 km or 17.4 miles

*'In Oranmore in the county Galway, one pleasant evening in the month of May'
from the traditional song' The Galway Shawl'*

The forecast today is for sunshine and showers, as our team of four start our run in Renville, Oranmore. Helen and Neill drive us there and park their campervan. Before we begin, we visit Renville Cemetery and remember Maureen's nephew Brendan who died suddenly in Australia in October 2021. Brendan had a passion for the sea and his headstone reflects this. From here in Renville, Brendan's parents Aideen and Kieran can see their own house across the bay. In the same way, from their home they can look across and see Renville cemetery.

We stick close to the shore running along country roads but suddenly we are recipients of the first heavy shower of the day. We take shelter under a tree and carry on through the light rain.

Helen doing some horse whispering

We follow a sign for Tawin Island which is easily crossed by a bridge. Even people in Galway city might not know exactly where Tawin is. The best way to explain its location is to say that, from Salthill you can see the island as you look across Galway Bay. It's that long stretch of land sitting in the middle of the bay, halfway between Galway and Clare.

As we're running along the island the heavy showers come down again. We meet a walker who stops to talk to us. Her name is Deirdre, and she tells us that she has a daughter, Gillian, in Rosedale Special School.

By the time we reach the end of the road on the western end of the island, we're soaked to the skin. We persevere even further along a trail and climb over a farmgate that brings us over a headland. We are rewarded with a unique view of Salthill across the bay.

Soaked to the skin at Old School House in Tawin

Tawin island – The Old School House

This small building stands at the end of the island and two very famous Irishmen met here for the first time. Eamon De Valera was director of the Summer School in Tawin and in 1912 Roger Casement came out to see how the school was doing. Casement was impressed, contributing towards prizes for a sports meeting. De Valera spent a few summers at the school and just recently, love letters that he wrote to his wife Sinead were discovered. *'There is a big vacancy in my heart. I feel empty, joyless without you'.* They were married for 65 years, and both died in 1975.

We leave Tawin and head back along the shore. Somehow, we have got separated from Sean which seems to be a regular occurrence when we run together. When we come to a T junction we are gladly reunited with Sean. We then must decide whether we go left along the country roads or take a right and try to find a trail that might lead to the coast. I convince the others to take the scenic (but rougher) route down to the shore. After all, it is a coastal run! The good news is that the weather is brightening up and our shirts are beginning to dry.

We trek through fields of long grass which is quite nice in the warm sunshine. We spot a farm gate, climb over, and run down to the shore and arrive at Ballinacourty Pier. Running along here is quite tricky on a very rocky coastline and trying to avoid the jellyfish.

Helen at Blackweir Pier, near Clarinbridge

Eventually we make it to another harbour, Blackweir Pier, and thankfully the terrain gets easier. We trample through a meadow looking for an exit to the shore. After climbing over some barbwire fences, we finally arrive at a coastal road a few miles west of Clarinbridge. We have reached civilisation again. Despite being chased by an angry dog along here, we finally made it to our finish line in the village of Clarinbridge.

STAGE 88

Co. Galway: Clarinbridge to Kinvara

Thursday 13 July 2023

29.5km or 18.3 miles

As I'm staying in Galway for the full week, I decide to get in a third coastal run. In the morning I take a short drive to Clarinbridge. The village is famous for its Oyster Festival and the person who started it all, seventy years ago, is Paddy Burke who runs one of the most famous pubs in this part of the world.

A grassy path in Stradbally, Clarinbridge

I run along the N67 for about 1km before taking a right into Stradbally North. This road comes to an end but I'm able to follow the shore on a grassy path until I link up with a lane on the south shore of the Dunkellin river (Stradbally South). There's another well-known oyster establishment here, *'Morans on the Weir'*.

I reach the village of Kilcolgan but take an immediate right (L8563) along the northern shore of the Dunkellin River and shortly I come to Kilcolgan Castle. The original structure dates as far back to the 11th century when it was a medieval castle, but it was rebuilt in 1801 by Christopher St George.

After a while I come to another huge building called Tyrone House, also built by St. George. Apparently, this was one of the grandest properties in Ireland. Visitors who entered the house were met by a life-size white marble statue of Lord St. George himself.

Tyrone House, Kilcolgan

I was able to walk through this shell of a building and imagine what life was like over two hundred years ago. During the Irish War of Independence in 1920, the house was burned down by the local Irish Republican Army. At that time the property was unoccupied, with just a caretaker who was bed-ridden, living there. He was carried from his bed and taken to another building on the premises before the building was set on fire.

I carry on along the country road and come to Killeenaran Pier. There are tractors on the shore today and men are collecting mussels and oysters for local markets. I rough it along the shore and eventually come to a field with a small family of cattle. It looks like a cow, a bull and two calves. The cow and calves scamper away but the bull stands in my way and stares at me. I decide to take a detour. Shortly I see a small monument on a hill, and I try to get closer, but I notice the marker is on a small island or inlet. It's called Knockapreaghaun (Hill of the crows).

After a while I come to an old water pump and follow a long boreen back down to the shore again to Pollagh Quay. I'm feeling very confident now as I can see Tarrea Pier just a few hundred metres along the shore. I know once I reach this harbour, it is a straightforward run into Kinvara. However, this short coastal section was quite a big challenge. I had to climb through thorny brambles and nettles, getting scratched and stung. After reaching the harbour, I run up to the main road (2km) and follow a convenient cycle lane all the way to Kinvara.

Nice to see this sign. It was a tough week of running

Arriving in Kinvara I run to the harbour and get to speak to a lady called Mary Moylan. As the two of us chat on the pier, she suddenly points *'that's my brother there'*. There was nobody else around, so I wondered what she was talking about. It turned out that there is a circular plaque on the wall at the end of the pier, dedicated to her brother, Anthony Moylan.

Plaque dedicated to Tony Moylan at Kinvara Harbour

Mary told me that Tony founded the famous *'Cruinniú na mBád'* boat festival in 1979. It is a celebration of the traditional commerce that existed between the coasts. Even though the rain was now starting to fall, I'm enjoying the interlude with Mary and her stories about the Moylan and Winkles family. Meanwhile her dog Lilly was getting great satisfaction from licking my legs. I believe it's the salty skin that he likes to taste. In any case I'm too exhausted to object after three long stages of coastal running this week.

STAGE 89

Kinvara, Co. Galway to New Quay, Co. Clare

Friday 15 Sept 2023

38.0 km or 23.6 miles

'Not time, nor tide, nor waters wide could wean my heart away. Forever true, it flies to you, my own dear Galway Bay'

Those lines are from the original *'Galway Bay'* and the best rendition is sung by the 'voice of traditional music' herself, Dolores Keane. The song was composed by Frank Fahy (1854-1935) a man who was native of Kinvara.

I returned to the pier at Kinvara where I finished my run in July and headed west. Passing St Colman's Church, I take a right and head down to Crushoa Pier. People told ghost stories about this area, but these tales were probably made up by locals to deter people stealing valuable oysters from nearby Mulroney's Island.

Heading north to 'Tawnagh East', I'm able to follow a grassy path shortcut, rather than going by Nogra. I reckon in olden times people followed this same route. I join up with the main road heading north just in time before it crosses over the sea towards Doorus.

Too late to make an offer - Sale Agreed

I could have easily missed Doorus House as it now seems to be in private ownership. The house was originally built in 1810 by a French man, de Basterot. Towards the end of the nineteenth century the family were friendly with Yeats and Lady Gregory and the idea for the Abbey Theatre was conceived here on the shores of Galway Bay.

In 1961 the house was given over to **'An Oige'**, the Irish Youth Hostel Association. I actually stayed here sometime in the 1980's when all the youth hostels in Ireland were in rural locations. In those days you could stay in an 'Oige Hostel' for a small charge, but you were also given a chore to do. I remember one of my tasks in Doorus House was to sweep the stairs.

Just another five hundred metres after Doorus House I see a sign for Parkmore cemetery. A grassy dirt track takes me down to an ancient graveyard with a medieval church. I arrive down near the shore and follow the coast all the way to Parkmore Pier. In Irish it is called *'Caladh na Sceiche'* which means 'hidden harbour'. The pier was built in 1881 when the main harbour in Kinvara was falling into disrepair. In my wisdom I decide to stay by the shore to reach Tracht Beach, but the grassy path soon disappeared. After that I was struggling through rocks that got bigger and bigger. It turned out to be my slowest kilometre of the day at 11.38 minutes.

A coastal path to Tracht Beach that disappears quickly

Saint Ciaran studied under St Enda on Aran Islands and when he went to set up his own monastery here at Tracht, *'a miraculous road opened up on the seabed'*. There's no sign of that miraculous road but in fairness to Ciaran, he did achieve a lot in his young life. In 544 he founded Clonmacnoise, a very famous monastery on the banks of the river Shannon.

I continue along Tracht strand and shortly arrive at Paradise Harbour. It doesn't seem very exotic on a dull cloudy day like today. I head slightly inland and followed a country road that brings me all the way to Aughinish Island.

Aughinish Island (Horse Island)

This causeway to the island was built in 1811 to service troops at the Martello Tower. At the tower itself, there are also a few additions; a metal stairway up to the doorway and two chimneys at the top, which look very peculiar.

I see a man with a bucket, and he tells me that he is collecting periwinkles. These marine creatures are really sea-snails and are very common on the rocky shores of Co. Clare.

There are high cliffs on the western tip of the island which make it impossible to stay by the coast. I climb up onto the headland and there's a long meadow in front of me. I see a herd of cattle in another field and try to avoid them but one or two spot me and start running in my direction. Lucky for me there are electric fences separating the fields.

The story is that Aughinish (Horse Island) was connected to the mainland near the Flaggy Shore until 1755. In that year there was a great tsunami in Portugal which even had an impact in the west of Ireland and separated Aughinish from the mainland on the south side. Standing here on the island and looking across to New Quay about 200 metres away, I find it hard to believe that only 268 years ago the island was connected to the mainland. Maybe 20,000 years ago! In any case the island is now linked to the mainland by a bridge on the east side. However, to get from Aughinish (Co. Clare) to other parts of Co. Clare you must go through Co. Galway.

The writer Thomas Cook, who I suspect was the famous travel agent, referred to this Redbank area with its coral weeds that have a reddish colour. He was here in 1842 and became quite excited when he saw some local ladies working on the shore.

'It is not unusual to see one hundred and fifty girls employed on the oyster beds here. These young women form a picturesque corps of mermaids, when seen paddling in the

shallow water, with red petticoats tucked up as high as their knees, and sometimes even higher.'

I leave the island (back into Co. Galway again) and follow a proper road along the coast. I pass near the Travellers Inn at Nogra, and eventually come back to the main road. I wasn't looking forward to running on the N67 and it was every bit as difficult as I suspected. I've had to deal with some dodgy experiences on my coastal run but running along a narrow busy road like the N67 equals any danger I've encountered.

I decide to get off the main road and take a left up a steep hill (L1014) and follow a *'green road'* which runs parallel to the N67. This trail is part of the route to *'Cnoc na Mainistreach'*. I've already run 30km today and light misty rain is beginning to fall. In hindsight, taking this green hilly boreen wasn't such a good idea. I'm struggling up the hills and I've now added another 90 metres (or 300 feet) of elevation.

I spot the main road down below and decide to make a deep descent through the steep fields. Once I'm back on the N67, I see the sign for New Quay and Linnane's Lobster Bar. Maureen, her sister Aideen, and our Brian are already there sitting at the table in the restaurant. I join them and settle for some tasty Seabass, washed down with a pint of Guinness.

Stage 88: Revisited: Sunday 10 March 2024: Island Eddy, Co. Galway: 8.7 km or 5.4 miles.

'A dear little island stands on Galway Bay. Not far from the pier which is called the Aran Quay. One look at its beauty, one row around its shore would make you regret living inland 'ere more'. (poem found in pocket of John Conlon, a native of Island Eddy, after he died in Boston in the 1900s)

Even those living in Galway know little about Island Eddy or where exactly it is situated. The island is easiest approached by taking the quiet L8563 from Kilcolgan. It was a long and winding road from the village and after about 5km I took a right turn (not signposted) down to Kileenaran Pier (or Aran Quay as its locally called). There are only a few windows of opportunities to reach Island Eddie on foot. This weekend was one of only two occasions this year when it was possible to get across at low tide. I wasn't taking any chances with the tide and so I contacted Brian Martyn who has a house on the island.

It's always so important to check with local knowledge before taking any risk as regards tide times. Brian met me at the pier and introduced me to his wife Helen who kindly volunteered to be my guide for the morning.

At the harbour I met a lovely couple Rena and John Deely and together with Helen our escort we walked along the shore for about one kilometre until we came to the point to cross over to the island. We waited there at this spot for about ten minutes, watching as the causeway slowly appeared out of the water, until it was finally safe to walk across. This long sandy path that leads to the island is known as **'the cush'**. Helen explained that there used to be seven families on Eddy, but the last people left as recently as the 1980's. However, during Covid, Helen and Brian Martyn moved to the island and now live alternatively between here and the mainland. The Martyns are also reviving an old traditional on the island. They grow vegetables and the only fertiliser they use is natural seaweed. Traditionally the produce from the island was always well respected and usually got the best prices at markets. When I met Brian on the pier, he handed me some of his Queen new potatoes and I confirm they are quite tasty.

An interesting fact about Island Eddy is that the body of man, Lindon Bates was washed up on the island on 30 July 1915 and found by John Conlon. Bates was a passenger on the Lusitania, which had been torpedoed by a German U-boat three months previously. The Lusitania sank a few hundred miles south, off the coast of Co. Cork. Its sinking turned public opinion against Germany and probably lead to America entering WW1. Lindon Bates was on deck on the Lusitania when the ship was hit and spent time helping Amy and Warren Pearl search for their three missing children. All five of the Pearl family survived the disaster, but unfortunately Lindon did not. The ship sunk in eighteen minutes. I'm not sure if the John Condon mentioned in the poem above, is the same man who found the body of Lindon Bates.

Once crossing *'the cush'* and arriving on the island, I set off running. In any case it was getting quite cold, so it was the perfect way to warm up. I did a short loop of the island and as I trampled through some lush and fertile looking grass, I understood why there is such a good tradition of vegetable growing. After my run I arrived back at the centre of the island and there met a group of local runners, led by Noel Gorman, who had taken advantage of today's extra low tide.

'Enjoying coffee in Helen Martyn's house on Island Eddy'

Helen and Brian's house is also here, and Helen invited Rena, John, and I into her lovely home. She even made coffee for us which was most welcome on a chilly day like today. I'm so grateful to Helen and Martin for giving me the opportunity to visit their *'dear little island'*.

So, this was the final piece of the jigsaw to finish the coast of Connacht. It's taken me four years to complete this province, although Covid did interrupt my adventure and restricted my travels.

I've always admired the writer, Tim Robinson who not only walked the coast of Connemara but mapped it all too. I understand his sentiments when he writes.

'I go to absurd lengths to complete the jigsaw puzzle. It seemed to me necessary to go everywhere and see everything before I had the right to represent anything in my drawing'.

In the same way, I don't like to miss any sections of the coast and I will often return to revisit a peninsula or a tidal island. I like to make sure I cover every corner of the coast.

To Hell or to Connacht: The West's Awake

I couldn't write a book about Connacht without mentioning the famous phrase, *'To Hell or to Connacht'*. People associate these words with Oliver Cromwell, but he had already left Ireland in 1654 when the great migration to Connacht began. The exodus to the western province was mainly made by Catholic Landowners from Ulster and other areas. These landowners were expelled from Ulster as a backlash to a massacre of 4,000 protestant settlers in 1641. This was later exaggerated to 154,000 and used to bring in laws to expel the Catholic landowners. Today **'To Hell or Connacht'** is often used in a defiant way. Almost saying to the rest of the country, we might have the wildest and most barren land in Ireland (and only 8% of the total Irish population), but we're still as good as any province. When Galway won the All-Ireland Football final in 1998 the Galway captain, Ray Silke mentioned this phrase. It was an important symbolic moment bringing the cup over the Shannon into the province of Connacht.

The traditional song, *'The West's Awake'* is in a similar mode. Thomas Davis, one of the United Irishmen, wrote this in the nineteenth century. He was impressed by a famous battle in Co. Mayo in 1798 where a combination of Frenchmen and Connacht men outwitted and out fought a stronger army. It became known as *'The Races of Castlebar'* as the enemy were sent galloping away. The Frenchman, General Humbert then proclaimed the 'Republic of Connacht' and declared the province was a 'client state of the French Republic'. Years later, in 1980, the late Joe McDonagh sang 'The West's Awake' in Croke Park to celebrate Galway's All-Ireland Hurling win.

> *Alas and well may Erin weep that Connacht lies in slumber deep. But hark, a voice like thunder spake, The West's awake. The West's awake!*

Epilogue

It's hard to believe that I have now completed all the coast of Ulster and now Connacht. That's 3,335km (or 2,072miles) so far. What started as a crazy idea, to run around the perimeter of Co. Down, escalated into a six-year project which ended up with me following the Irish coast, north and west to the southern shores of Galway Bay. So far there's been a few scary moments in my adventure, some strange encounters, all kinds of extreme weather and a few wrong turns along the way. I pushed my body to the limit, struggled and suffered on many occasions but I always got there in the end!

And the adventure continues into Co. Clare and the rest of Munster. According to Neilson & Costello, Munster's coastline is 2,176km (1,352 miles), the longest shoreline of the four provinces. I realise that it's going to take me further from my home in Bangor, Co. Down and I'll probably have to plan some weekly trips to Kerry and Cork. See my blog to follow my progress in the months and years ahead. https://cliftoncoastalrun.blogspot.com/

Still, it is an achievable challenge and I realise I'm lucky and privileged to have the energy to continue this journey. I don't know the true length of the Irish coastline or even how long it will take me to complete it all. I'm not sure how difficult it will be, what obstacles might lie ahead and if my long-suffering legs will continue to thrive. However, every time I start a new run, I'm as excited as the nineteen-year-old, Laurie Lee, when he started his adventure. In his book, *'As I Walked Out One Midsummers Morning'* Laurie describes his feelings when he left his home in Gloucestershire.

> *'I was affronted by freedom. The day's silence said, 'Go where you will. It's all yours. You asked for it. You're on your own, and nobody's going to stop you'. I was excited, knowing I had far to go; but not, as yet how far'*

Coast of Connacht - Stage by Stage

Stage	Mth	Start	Finish		Km	Miles
41	Feb-20	Bundoran	Grange	via Mullaghmore & Cliffony Beach	27.0	16.8
42	Feb-20	Grange	Drumcliff	via Raghly Point & Lissadell Beach	34.4	21.4
42	Feb-20	Streedagh	Grange	via Conor's Island	14.8	9.2
43	Feb-20	Drumcliff	Sligo Town	via Rosses Point	22.6	14.0
44	Feb-20	Sligo Town	Ballysadare	via Strandhill & Culleenamore Strand	31.3	19.4
44	Sep-20	*Revisited*	*Coney Island*	Circle of island	13.1	8.1
45	Mar-20	Ballysadare	Dromore West	via Streamstown & Dunmoran Strand	40.3	25.0
46	Mar-20	Dromore West	Ballina	via Inishcrone beach & Lenadoon Point	48.4	30.1
47	Aug-20	Ballina	Rathlachan	via Killala & Humbert 1798 trail	41.2	25.6
47	Sep-23	Revisited	Bartragh Island	Circle of Bartragh Island	14.1	8.8
48	Sep-20	Rathlachan	Belderrig	via Dunbriste & Downpatrick Head	37.7	23.4
49	Jun-21	Belderrig	A. Brady Bridge	via Porturlin, Portacloy & Carrowteige	50.0	31.1
50	Jun-21	A. Brady Bridge	Belmullet Town	via Pullathomas, Inver & Strand	35.8	22.2
51	Jul-21	Clogher, Mullet	Ballyglass L/Hs.	via Rosbarnagh Island & Belmullet town	46.3	28.8
52	Jul-21	L/house	Tra Bheal Doire	via Tipp Pier, Erris Head & Annagh Head	39.5	24.5
53	Jul-21	Tra Bheal Doire	Tra Deirbhile	via coastal beaches (west Mullet)	17.2	10.7
54	Jul-21	Tra Deirbhile	Clogher, Mullet	via an Mullach Rua beach	13.7	8.5
55	Aug-21	Belmullet	Gaoth Saile	via Claggan Island & Doolough Strand	41.0	25.5
56	Aug-21	Gaoth Saile	Bangor Erris	via Doohoma peninsula and beach	34.0	21.1
57	Aug-21	Bangor Erris	Ballycroy	via Carrigeenmore and Fahy/Doona	45.7	28.4

57	Sep-23	Revisited	Inis Bigil	via Annagh Island and across long strand	11.8	7.3
58	Aug-21	Ballycroy	Achill Sound	via Bellacragher & Mullranny	37.0	23.0
59	Sept-21	Achill Sound	Mullranny	via south coast of Corraun Peninsula	29.7	18.4
60	Sep-21	Achill Sound	Doogort	via Dooinver Beach & Golden Strand	34.6	21.5
61	Sep-21	Doogort	Keel Strand	via Slievemore, Annagh & Keem Strands	36.7	22.8
61	Jun-23	Revisited, Croaghaun Cliffs		via Acorrymore, Achill Head & Moyteoge	16.6	10.3
62	Sep-21	Keel Strand	Achill Sound	via Dooega and Cloughmore	31.1	19.3
63	Feb-22	Mullranny	Newport	via Rosmore Point & Lough Furnace	28.6	17.8
64	Feb-22	Newport	Rosmoney Pier	via Kilmeena & cycle loop	15.5	9.6
65	Feb-22	Rosmoney Pier	Westport	via Inishcottle, Inishnakillew & Collan	14.5	9.0
66	Mar-22	Westport	Louisburgh	via Mullisk, Croagh Patrick & Old Head	38.4	23.9
67	Mar-22	Louisburgh	Louisburgh	via Roonah, White&Silver Strand & Killadoon	43.0	26.7
68	Apr-22	Louisburgh	Leenane	via Famine Road/Doolough	31.3	19.4
69	Apr-22	Leenane	Tully Cross	via Rosroe Pier & south shore of Killary	34.4	21.4
70	May-22	Tully Cross	Cleggan	via Renvyle Point & Tully Mountain	43.6	27.1
70	Aug-22	Revisited	Cleggan Cliffs	loop of peninsula	11.4	7.1
71	May-22	Cleggan	Clifden	via Rossadillask and Aughrusbeg Lough	24.0	14.9
71	Sep-23	Revisited	Omey Island	via Hillock of the women & Cnoc an Bhiora	11.0	6.8
72	Jun-22	Clifden	Ballyconneely	via Sky Road & Alcock&Brown memorials	42.6	26.5
73	Jun-22	Ballyconneely	Ballyconneely	via Knock Hill, Doonloughan&Golf Course	24.4	15.2

73	Aug-22	Revisited	Slyne Head	loop of peninsula	9.1	5.7
74	Sep-22	Ballyconneely	Roundstone	via Murvey, Dogs Bay & Gorteen point	22.7	14.1
75	Sep-22	Pre-Visit	Rosroe	loop of peninsula	16.0	9.9
75	Sep-22	Pre-Visit	Inishnee Island	loop of island	12.0	7.5
75	Sep-22	Roundstone	Glynsk	via Aillenacally and Lehenagh	28.1	17.5
76	Oct-22	Glynsk	Cill Chiarain	via Mairois, Mace Head & Loch na gCaor	31.7	19.7
76	Oct-22	Revisited	Mweenish	via Roisin na Chalaidh Island	13.4	8.3
76	Mar-24	Revisited	Finish Island	Loop from Tigh Leavys Pub & across the sand	12.9	8.0
77	Oct-22	Cill Chiarain	Rosmuc	along R340 as far as Pearse's Cottage	14.6	9.1
78	Feb-23	Rosmuc Peninsula		Loop of peninsula	35.2	21.9
79	Feb-23	Rosmuc	Beal an Daingin	Via Camus and Muiceanach Shaile	27.1	16.8
80	Feb-23	Beal an Daingin	Leitir Mor	via Islands of Leitir Mor & Eanach Mheain	28.8	17.9
81	Mar-23	Gorumna Island		via Tra Bhain & Bothar na Oilean	32.8	20.4
81	May-23	Revisited	Ballynakill Church and Graveyard - loop via coast		3.8	2.4
82	May-23	Circling Leitir Mullan Island		via Golam Head, An Crapach & Foirnis	14.1	8.8
83	May-23	Beal an Daingin	Casla (Costello)	via An Cheathru Peninsula & Oilean na Rossa	39.1	24.3
84	May-23	Casla	Spiddal	via Rossaveel &sticking to shore all the way	33.6	20.9
85	May-23	Spiddal	Salthill	via shore, Silver Strand & Gentian Hill	20.8	12.9
86	Jul-23	Salthill	Oranmore	via Mutton Isl., Cathedral & Ballyloughane	32.1	19.9
86	Mar-24	Revisited	Hare Island	From Ballyloughane Beach in Renmore	4.7	2.9
87	Jul-23	Oranmore	Clarinbridge	via Renville, Tawin Isl. & Ballinacourty Pier	28.0	17.4
88	Jul-23	Clarinbridge	Kinvara	via Stradbally Nth&Sth & Killeenaran Pier	29.5	18.3

88	Mar-24	Revisited	Island Eddy	From Killeenaran Pier near Kilcolgan	8.7	5.4
89	Sept-23	Kinvara	New Quay	via Doorus, Tracht & Aughinish Island	38.0	23.6
				Total Connacht Mileage	1,745	1,084
				Plus, Province of Ulster Mileage	1,590	988
				Total mileage so far around the coast of Ireland	3,335	2,072
					kms	miles

www.ingramcontent.com/pod-product-compliance
Lightning Source LLC
Chambersburg PA
CBHW051330110526
44590CB00032B/4467